Y0-BQG-207

Slaves of the Machine

Slaves of the Machine
The Quickening of Computer Technology

Gregory J. E. Rawlins

The empires of the future are the empires of the mind.
Winston Churchill, *Onwards to Victory*

A Bradford Book
The MIT Press
Cambridge, Massachusetts
London, England

Second printing, 1998
© 1997 Gregory J. E. Rawlins

This book was set in Sabon by Windfall Software using ZzTEX.

Printed and bound in the United States of America.

Library of Congress Cataloging-in-Publication Data

Rawlins, Gregory J. E.
  Slaves of the machine : the quickening of computer technology /
Gregory J. E. Rawlins
    p. cm.
  "A Bradford book."
  Includes index.
  ISBN 0-262-18183-5 (hardcover : alk. paper)
  1. Computers and civilization.   2. Computers—History.   I. Title.
QA76.9.C66R395   1997
004—dc21
                                                      97-4013
                                                        CIP

To the next generation,
Both human and machine.

I died from a mineral and plant became
Died from the plant, took a sentient frame;
Died from the beast, donned a human dress—
When by my dying did I ever grow less?
Jalaluddin Rumi

Contents

Preface

The whole question comes down to this: Can the human mind master what the human mind has made?

Paul Valéry

When I was young, computers were far off and extravagantly expensive. No ordinary person, I thought, could actually own one, far less understand one. I had only heard them mentioned on my visits to the bank (I was a thrifty child) and in overheard snatches of my parents' conversations: "The computer sent us this bill," and "Oh dear, what'll we do about this computer card?" and "Oops, I've bent it. Will it still work, do you think?"

I'd also seen a few of them on television—room-filling machines surrounded by worshipful supplicants and dozens of grim, crewcut engineers. Obviously, using these mythic devices, never mind understanding them, was for the privileged few with power and wealth. To compound my confusion, I'd heard that the important part of the computation was done in (or was it by?) silicon. Silicon, I knew from science class, was the main ingredient of rocks and sand.

So how could a rock think?

One day at the beach, sitting on the hot sand, I realized I was surrounded by tons of silicon. What had happened to change sand, apparently good only for digging in and lying on, into these amazing machines? It was then I knew I wanted to read a book like this.

This book is my attempt to explain to my younger self what computers are and where they're going. Each chapter addresses a simple question: "What are computers?" "How do we build them?" "How do we talk to them?" "Why is programming them hard?" "What can't they do?" "Could they think?" Each chapter carries its topic all the way from its historical beginnings to the state of the art as of 1997, and on into the future.

This book also touches on some of the most fundamental questions of human life: What are we? What do we value? Where are we going? Our earliest uses of computers predetermined their structure and what we could—or should—do with them. Our choices today are both narrowed and widened by those shortsighted choices we made decades ago, and our choices today are similarly going to influence our choices tomorrow. Ultimately, the future development of computer technology will determine whether we continue to exist as organic beings or evolve into something other.

This book is for you if you don't know much about computers and want to know what they can do for you—or to you. It tells the story of how we became slaves to our silicon dependents, and how they may one day become slaves to us.

Read it at the beach.

1

A Strange New Machine

Know from whence you came. If you know from whence you came there's really no limit on where you can go.
James Baldwin

Everything that we see is a shadow cast by that which we do not see.
Martin Luther King, Jr., *The Measure of Man*

Never was any such event so inevitable yet so completely unforeseen.
Alexis de Tocqueville, *The Old Regime and the Revolution*

What are computers? A computer professional might answer that question with something technical, like "They are universal information manipulators," an answer that is about as useful as saying that hair driers are moisture manipulators. What does manipulating information mean—and how can a machine do it?

Let's try an easier question first. How does an automatic toaster know when to eject the bread? Most toasters have a bent piece of wire heating up along with the bread. When the wire gets hot enough, it touches another one, completing a circuit and ejecting the bread. Other toasters have a spring timer or computer chip that does the same thing. Every automatic toaster, however made, must have some way to make simple decisions.

And so do computers. The big difference is that, unlike toasters, computers can string enormous numbers of simple decisions together to do quite complex things. Of course, just making simple decisions doesn't make them smart. Nor does it mean that they have desires, emotions, or common sense. They're automatic machines that do our bidding even when we're not watching over them. They don't so much save labor as save attention.

That piece of bent wire in the toaster (or the spring timer, or the computer chip) is manipulating a tiny piece of information that tells it when to break the circuit and eject the bread. It's an alarm clock. A clock could tick off seconds forever, but an alarm clock always has to, in effect, keep asking itself "Should I ring now?" Similarly, a wood stove simply heats up, but a gas oven always has to ask "Am I warm enough now?" In a primitive way, they both have to decide something. In other words, they too are rudimentary information manipulators, though not computers. So are thermostats and bombs. Imagine how useless bombs would be if they blew up any old time.

From ovens to spaceships, from mousetraps to nuclear power stations, we're surrounded by millions of automatic devices each containing small gobs of congealed wisdom. These devices don't "think," but they act as if they do. Toasters don't sit up nights thinking about how to toast our bread in the morning, but the consequence of their actions is perfectly toasted bread for us to eat.

These gobs of wisdom scattered all over the landscape give us power. Instead of washing our clothes by hand, for example, we use machines with built-in clothes-washing cycles that represent the distilled wisdom of many expert clothes washers. Or take music boxes and player pianos. The rotating barrel with its irregularly placed rows of pins making the music represents information gleaned from musicians—it is information made tangible.

Once information is tangible, machines can manipulate it. The computer is the ultimate artificial information manipulator. Unlike other devices, we can teach it to manipulate any information we can describe clearly enough. So we can make it do one thing one day, then something completely different the next. That versatility is what makes it a universal information manipulator.

Once upon a time, people had to direct traffic through all busy intersections, switch all telephone calls, operate all elevators, and dispense all banked money. Now computers do much of that decision making for us. They help design, build, then operate our cars, our microwave ovens, our communications systems. They help manage our businesses, our governments, our very lives. How is that possible? Why are they such universal machines?

Tinkertoy Computers

Hydroelectric dams and jumbo jets have to be big and expensive to do their jobs, but computers don't. Year by year, they get smaller and faster and cheaper; and, year by year, they do more. Unlike other machines, they don't so much manipulate force, energy, or matter as ideas.

Ideas aren't physical, and making them tangible so that machines can manipulate them can take very little energy. That's why we can make computers ever smaller, faster, and cheaper. Each new computer generation uses less energy to manipulate more ideas than the last one. Thinking takes energy, of course, but it needn't take much. The ultimate "computer," our own brain, uses only ten watts of power—one-tenth the energy consumed by a hundred-watt light bulb.

Since we use computers primarily as idea manipulators, not as doorstops or room heaters, how we happen to build them today isn't very important. Today's computers are electronic, but that's irrelevant. The same work could be done—more slowly, less reliably, more expensively—by almost anything: valves and water pipes, toothed wheels and brass rods, even a child's set of Tinkertoys.

In 1979 some students at the Massachusetts Institute of Technology actually built an information manipulator with Tinkertoys—wooden sticks and spools with holes in them. Their machine played tic-tac-toe (naughts and crosses), and they built it from thirty boxes of Tinkertoys, some cabling, an axle, and a hand crank. The whole contraption looked like a huge upended abacus mated to an upside-down suspension bridge. It didn't use electricity, have a screen or a keyboard, and it never varied what it did. When its operator cranked it up and gave it a tic-tac-toe position by setting some little switches, the suspension bridge part of it slowly fell, clicking its way down until it found its built-in move for that position.

So it was an information manipulator—it made decisions as it operated—but it didn't really *play* tic-tac-toe. It reacted in a fixed, knee-jerk way to each position it found itself in. It didn't work automatically or follow moves in sequence. And, since an operator had to crank it up after every tic-tac-toe move, it certainly didn't save attention. Nor was it a computer—we'll see why in a moment—though anyone with an awful lot of time (and an awful lot of Tinkertoys) could build a real computer out of Tinkertoys. Of course, it would probably be as big as a barn, and would probably take several months to do anything useful. Still, it would do what any computer does, which is manipulate arbitrary information. That's the important thing.

Taxation with Representation

Every year, the government forces each of us to follow their printed instructions and complete a tax form. If we're foolhardy enough to tackle the task alone, we might first fetch our income records, bills, and other documents—perhaps from a big box in the basement. Then we might settle ourselves comfortably at a desk and read the instructions carefully to see what we have to do this year. Once we've read as much as we can stand, we find the information in our records, do some arithmetic, and write the results on the form. Of course, we do more than fill out tax forms all year long, but in this one area, we and today's computers are the same. Each of us at tax time is a *processor* mindlessly following a list of rigid, prespecified instructions.

So if we buy a computer to help us do our taxes, it too must have some kind of processor; these days that's usually a thumbnail-sized computer chip. Also, it needs a device to let us see a representation of the tax form; these days that's usually a screen. And it should have some device letting us give it information and instructions; these days that's generally a keyboard. The keyboard replaces our pen, the screen replaces our paper, and the chip replaces our brain. The computer should also have some kind of scratchpad to use, as we might use a piece of paper, to scribble our tax calculations. And it should have somewhere to store things for a long time, just as we might keep tax records in a big dusty box in the basement.

The tax instructions we have to follow may be complex but, presumably, they're precise—because the consequences of not following them to the letter are grave. Every step has to be clearly defined, and the instructions need to cover all cases. Computer people might call creating the list of tax instructions *programming*. Each program, whether it's the program the revenue people write (the list of tax instructions) or the program we run to fill in the form, is a piece of *software*. Anything we can touch in the computer system, like the keyboard or the screen, is *hardware*. Computer folk love to generalize; so anything promised but nonexistent—like simple and clear tax laws—is *vaporware*.

We can see now why neither a toaster, nor a time bomb, nor even the MIT students' Tinkertoy tic-tac-toe machine is a computer. They're all information manipulators of one kind or another—that is, they all make decisions—but they're all single purpose. They can't run any program we want, whenever we want; their behavior can't change easily. Time bombs can't play show tunes, player pianos can't make toast, toasters can't explode (well, not usually anyway). None of them could play chess, analyze music, do our taxes, direct traffic, or run a lawn mower. Computers, though, can do all these things, all at the same time.

Computers are something new. They aren't crosses between television sets and typewriters that only do arithmetic or word processing. That just happens to be what most of them look like today. Instead, they're idea machines. They are devices that can be taught how to follow any information process we can describe very precisely. Their principal physical parts let them read, write, remember, and modify arbitrary information. The technology carrying out those four tasks twenty years from now will be vastly different from today's primitive mechanisms, just as a tiny computer chip is different from a barnful of Tinkertoys. But that doesn't matter. The basic idea will be the same. Probably.

The Little Engine That Could've

Perhaps the best way to understand computers is to think about how they developed. Nineteenth-century England is as good a place to start as any. In 1823, Napoleon was but two years dead, the future Queen Victoria was four years old, and the United States Army was busy fighting Native Americans in Illinois. In London, England, an obscure mathematician and inventor named Charles Babbage had just designed a calculating engine. At a time when most Britons couldn't read and arithmetic was almost a secret art, Babbage was one of the first to see that machines could do jobs having nothing to do with muscle power. He dreamt of an all-purpose calculating engine, like the marvelous steam engine then busily driving the industrial revolution. First, though, he started with an engine to calculate automatically certain numerical tables. Such an engine, he thought, could be cheaper, faster, and far more reliable than the hordes of mathematicians then compiling these tables.

Why stop with calculating the tables, though? Why not have the engine etch copper printing plates directly rather than typesetting the results by hand? Numerical tables in those days were full of errors, and typesetter mistakes only compounded the calculators' errors. Babbage saw that the only human effort needed would be to design and maintain the engine.

Babbage also had a ready-made task for his proposed engine. He planned to sell the idea of cheap and flawless tables of longitudes, tides, and so forth to the Royal Navy. In those days, about a thousand ships a year went aground because of faulty tables and too few lighthouses. If his engine saved only two or three ships it would more than pay back its cost.

The machine would be easy to use too. The operator would only have to prime the pump, so to speak, with a few numbers. The engine would then automatically produce a long stream of accurate numbers—calculated by addition only—like so many sausages from a sausage maker. And, ever-courteous, it would obligingly print the table as it produced it. As Babbage said then, error-free tables would be as cheap as potatoes.

A few farsighted military men, including the first Duke of Wellington—a future prime minister and Napoleon's conqueror at Waterloo—saw the engine's importance not only for navigation but also for artillery and naval gunnery. Despite a total lack of comprehension by everyone else in the government, they pushed through an initial grant of fifteen hundred pounds, a sum that in 1823 could feed a large family—including servants—for life.

Babbage worked on his engine off and on for eleven years, during which time his wife and two of their children died. Then he abandoned it. Like many latter-day computer people, he had had a brilliant new idea for a machine that would eclipse the old one. He had dreamt the computer.

The Dream Machine

The idea for what we would today call the first true computer came to Babbage eleven years later, in 1834. Abraham Lincoln entered politics that year as an unknown assemblyman in the Illinois legislature, his fateful presidency still twenty-seven years in the future. America still kept slaves. Only the year before had slavery finally been abolished within the British Empire. Babbage, however, was designing a new kind of slave, using an idea he stole from economics—the division of labor.

At first, Babbage only wanted to build a machine that could do any kind of arithmetic whatsoever. As a part-time political economist, he knew that the division of labor guides the design of everything from houses to factories to the world's economy. For example, we put everything to do with food in kitchens, everything to do with sleep in bedrooms, and so on. So when designing his all-purpose arithmetical engine, division of labor told him not to try to do everything everywhere.

First, he needed a way to store numbers—a memory. For that he used upright brass columns with equidistant vertical rows of toothed wheels like the numbered wheels on a combination lock. The technical details don't matter. We can just as well think of his brass columns with gears as labeled boxes holding numbers. Second, he needed a processor to do arithmetic. But, for simplicity, and again consonant with the division of labor, he designed the processor to work not on the numbers in every box in memory but only on those in two special boxes that were near it. Third, he needed some way to fetch numbers from memory and send them to the processor. For that he invented a contraption that would copy a number from any other box to the two special ones, and vice versa.

With these three fairly simple parts, he could put numbers in the machine's memory, fetch any two numbers, do arithmetic on them, and store the result back in memory. Because the boxes were labeled—like a line of mailboxes—his engine always knew where to find everything.

Without his insight into the importance of dividing labor, his engine would have been both unthinkable and unbuildable. Which is why we design today's computers largely the same way, even though his ideas were forgotten for a hundred years. Still, although the division of labor is important, it wasn't quite enough to make a computer. For that Babbage needed something simple, but outrageous.

Eating Your Own Tail

Dividing labor was Babbage's first idea. Even so, his processor design was pretty complicated because he first thought he would have to build separate pieces of machinery to add, subtract, multiply, divide, and do all other more complex arithmetical operations. There would be thousands of handmade parts for each complex function. At this point he nearly gave up. He knew he couldn't build anything that elaborate.

His problem was that in the world of physical engines—which was all he and everyone else in the nineteenth century knew—the more things we ask an engine to do, the more complicated it becomes. A steam shovel is one thing, but a steam shovel that can vacuum carpets while playing the piccolo is something else again. It's easy enough to build something to add two numbers, but then to multiply them seems to need more machinery. To divide them seems to need yet more; and to do more complex things, a vast quantity more. But Babbage was clever. He knew that multiplication is just repeated addition and that division is just repeated subtraction. It turns out that we can convert all other numerical operations into sequences of additions and subtractions. We can even reduce subtraction to addition.

Babbage was also the first to see that besides the ability to add, a general computing engine only needs a way to test whether one number is bigger than another and a way to repeat instructions. It's that simple. We can replace any computer, no matter how complex, by another that only follows long sequences of just three simple instructions: add, test, and repeat. Conversely, anything that can follow these simple directions is a computer just as powerful as any other, although perhaps not as fast.

Babbage's genius didn't stop there. While he was busy simplifying his processor, he stumbled on another important idea. Besides punching little cards to get numbers into memory, he gave his engine the power to punch its own instruction cards, then read and act on them later if it needed to. Thus his engine could change its own behavior *after* it was started. Babbage called that "the engine eating its own tail," evoking the ancient myth of the Worm Ouroboros, a World Serpent with its tail in its mouth—eating itself to produce itself.

Since Babbage could break down any numerical operation into a long sequence of a few simple operations, he realized that he didn't have to build a lot of complicated parts at all. He had but to build a few simple parts, then figure out how to do each task using sequences of the few fixed operations these parts could carry out. The engine could punch that sequence into cards, then read and follow the punched sequence. That tremendous insight let Babbage simplify his processor design enormously. He saw that not only could he talk to his engine, he could make it *talk to itself*. He had invented programming.

An engine that could modify its own behavior while it was running, talking to itself and continually reinventing itself in the form currently needed, was a new idea in the history of the world. Nothing like such an infinitely reprogrammable device existed before Babbage conjured it up. And from it followed consequences in numberless profusion.

For one thing, the important part of his engine was not the hardware—the higgledy-piggledy pile of brass and pewter clockwork he used to build it—but the punch cards telling it what to do—the software. Suddenly, machines could become almost insubstantial: a few physical parts doing a few simple things, with all the other actions programmed by software.

Babbage's final design had all the principal physical parts we identified in all modern computers: ways to manipulate information (a processor), read information (a card reader), write information (a printer and card punch), and remember information (columns with numbered wheels and previously punched cards). It would have been the size of a locomotive and been densely packed with high-precision gears, wheels, pewter clockwork, and brass rods. It would have run on steam. If built, it would have been the world's first computer. Alas, the world's first computer forever remained, in computer parlance, vaporware.

By 1842 successive British governments had sunk well over seventeen thousand pounds into Babbage's various projects. They would spend no more. After the first few years passed with no sign of a viable engine, the government ignored his pleas for more support, thinking his engine worthless. An engine to do mental work? The very idea was absurd.

Ignored by his country, Babbage died a bitter and reclusive old man on Wednesday, October 18, 1871. His stillborn machine then lay, forgotten, in bits and pieces in dusty libraries for a hundred years. Yet, on Friday, November 29, 1991, two hundred years after his birth, his first engine—built with methods available in Victorian England—did its first full-scale calculation at the London Science Museum. Babbage could indeed have built his computing engine in the nineteenth century. If he had, the world would have been changed forever.

Brass and Iron

In the twentieth century another farsighted English mathematician also dreamt of machines that manipulated information. Alan Turing, like Babbage before him, was a brilliant and deeply original thinker. He carried his originality much further than Babbage did, however; he strove to be totally self-sufficient. Throughout his life, for example, he continually looked for ways to make common things—weed killer, bricks, soap, cleaning fluid—from household objects. He was determined to take nothing for granted, determined to be a Robinson Crusoe of the mind.

In 1935 he was attracted to a deep mathematical problem and brought to it his desert-island attitude—with spectacular success. Unaware of Babbage's work, Turing started from scratch, as always, and defined an abstract machine embodying the few essentials we've already identified in Babbage's design. His imaginary machine was a computer in all but name; that is, it could manipulate any information he could define precisely. In other words, like the computer Babbage never built, it could read, write, remember, and manipulate arbitrary information.

Turing proved that, given only these humble abilities, no information manipulator, no matter how it was made or what it could do, could be more powerful than his abstract machine. Other machines might work faster or cheaper, but none could do any more, no matter what set of basic actions it could perform.

Turing was one of the first to see that once we understand a process well enough to fully describe it to a computer, the computer can simulate the process. (Of course, that leaves out everything we don't fully understand, which, alas, is almost everything.) So, if we can fully describe the workings of any machine in a table of behaviors (in this case do this, in that case do that), we can make a computer simulate the machine by simply making it follow that table.

And that has bizarre consequences. For instance, usually we can distinguish a machine from the thing it works on: washing machines, for example, aren't clothes. Not so for computers. In the case of the computer, a table completely describing a machine's behavior *is* the machine. The table is the machine's software, but it is more than that; nothing important about the machine's behavior is not included in its software. For example, sending out tax instructions every year is the same as (but cheaper than) sending us each a physical machine for us to stick in our particular tax information, turn the crank, and pop out a completed tax form. By sending those instructions, the government essentially turns *us* into temporary tax machines. It's a wonder we don't rebel.

So, if we build something that does everything a typewriter or washing machine does, that's what it is, no matter what it looks like or what we planned when we built it. And, because what a computer does changes depending on what program it's running, it can become any machine we can imagine clearly enough. So, for computers, identity, as well as beauty, is in the beholder's eye. They're indeed strange new machines.

High Horse Riderless

At the outbreak of the Second World War in 1939, Turing went to work for his government, helping decrypt secret German radio messages. Luckily for the British, his job was made much easier because, apart from their skill at warmaking, Germany's leaders were still living in the previous century. The German High Command, despite many clues to the contrary, refused to believe that the secrecy game could change. They used a machine to encrypt secret messages, never imagining that the enemy might use a machine to decrypt them. Only people, they thought, could do that.

Still, they were doing quite well at waging war, and by 1940 Britain was in dire straits. Then Turing and his team of decrypters built a primitive kind of computer and, sitting poker-faced at the wartime card table, used it to read all Hitler's cards. The puzzled German generals never really understood what went wrong with their superb war machine.

It really doesn't matter how many U-boats you have, if your enemy always knows where they are. The Royal Air Force pilots were no doubt heroic, but without the decrypted messages and the newly invented radar to tell them when and where the next attack would come, Britain might not have survived to memorialize them. Without the new information technologies, more supply ships racing across the Atlantic from America would have been sunk, more planes ferrying bombs to Germany would have been shot down, and Britain probably would have been occupied in 1941.

Turing's work was so desperately important that Churchill took a strong interest in it, even coming to meet him personally. And, as Turing's group used their primitive device throughout 1942 to decrypt messages from Germany, they learned of a new, urgent reason to get better equipment: some of the intercepted messages spoke of trains, and showers, and industrial quantities of cyanide.

This Immense Power

Before war's end, Turing, like Babbage before him, saw that he could build a real version of his abstract all-purpose machine. All he needed was money. Once again, the British government was initially interested. Among other things, such a device would make it easy to decrypt secret messages from, say, a big Slavic country.

Alas, the postwar bureaucrats understood the machine's uses little better than their counterparts had a century before, when Babbage first talked about it. Although they funded Turing's project—hoping to beat the Americans to it—the country was exhausted, and ignorance and bureaucracy die hard. Nor can we really blame the officials for their immense failure of foresight. We're surely making similar mistakes today, and our descendants are going to laugh at us just as loudly as we laugh at our forebears. It's useful to recall, for instance, that women couldn't vote in Britain or America until the end of the First World War and that Swiss women had to wait until 1971. The world we know today is a very recent invention.

Even science fiction writers—those few who offered glimmers of our future—utterly failed to predict the computer or to foresee its consequences. The year before Babbage died, Jules Verne published *Twenty Thousand Leagues Under the Sea*, and for thirty-five more years he wrote about all sorts of absurdities: submarines, airplanes, television, telephones, fax machines, subways, guided missiles, moon shots, the electric chair. But a machine that could do mental work? That was simply too absurd, even for Verne.

As late as the 1950s, years after the first modern computers were developed, we could understand stronger ships and bigger tanks and faster planes—and perhaps even submarines and radar and rockets and nuclear power. Yet this new thing, this gossamer confabulation of information and intelligence, had no precedent. Having nothing to compare it to, we neither knew how to treat it nor what to expect from it. We still don't.

Like Babbage before him, Turing saw so far ahead that he never understood why he had to explain everything he foresaw to the government. He never realized that bureaucracy glaciates without the urgency of total war, or grasped that politics plays a more important role in our affairs than reason does. He didn't understand that despite the lip service we pay to it, we absolutely loath change. He was slowly squeezed out of his own project.

People are what they fight for. Bereft of his brainchild, Turing no longer had anything to fight for—nor anything to fight with. Then, in 1952, the British courts convicted him of homosexual acts, then a crime as serious as incest or necrophilia. He was ordered to undergo chemical castration by estrogen therapy, instead of a prison sentence or surgical castration. Among other things, the estrogen gave him breasts. He told close friends that he had lost all interest in his research.

In his twenties, Turing had been much taken with the Wicked Witch's couplet from Disney's *Snow White and the Seven Dwarfs*:

Dip the apple in the brew,
Let the Sleeping Death seep through.

Two weeks short of his forty-second birthday, on Monday, June 7, 1954, he ate an apple and went to sleep. Ever true to his desert-island mentality, he had made his own cyanide.

The Universe in a Shoebox

Most of us think of a computer as a machine much like any other—more unusual perhaps, capable of more things perhaps—but still a machine. It does some obscure and tedious calculations our ancestors were stupid enough to think were hard, but we know better. These things are so simple even a machine can do them. Or are they?

The answer to this question is not so clear, because the computer is a particularly strange new machine. It follows from Babbage's, then Turing's, thinking that we could build one with a loom, a player piano, even Tinkertoys. Unlike other machines, its physical parts almost don't matter. Once we give it the power to create arbitrary information it can later interpret—that is, once it has some way to talk to itself—it becomes programmable. By eating its own tail it becomes an all-purpose information manipulator. That isn't much like a belt sander or a tractor. What kind of machine is it?

Let's follow Turing's train of thought to one more station. As long as we can reinterpret instructions in one machine as text, why not use numbers as substitutes for things besides numbers—for example, words, colors, musical pitches? If we use Morse code, say, we can represent any information we can describe precisely. And, if we can represent any problem we can describe, and figure out exactly how to solve it step by tiny step, we can make a computer solve the problem too. (Of course, it might be a bit slow.) So if we're prepared to wait long enough, a computer can do anything we can precisely explain in simple actions—whether that's how to play tic-tac-toe, do tax forms, or run a space shuttle. Consequently, because it can run arbitrary software, a computer isn't one machine—it's every machine we can describe—it's a universal machine.

Because mathematicians and engineers invented it and warriors paid for it, it was first used for things that mathematicians, engineers, and warriors care about. If painters and writers had invented it and weavers had paid for it, it would have been used differently. But that doesn't matter. Eventually, it will be used by everyone for everything, although it will first have to become a lot more complicated.

Two thousand million years ago the brain was probably very simple, because that's how everything starts. Today though, that simple brain is buried beneath the shifting sands of evolutionary time and the brain is very complicated. It isn't designed from scratch the way today's computers are. Our brain is like a million-page book whose every sentence depends on every other sentence for its meaning. We'll eventually read it all, yet we may never fully understand it. That doesn't mean, though, that we couldn't one day make a machine to rival it.

Our complex and clever brain lets us do many amazing things that our current computers can't. It doesn't follow, however, that future computers won't ever become as smart as we are. Infants, too, know little of the world, yet they manage to learn a lot by the time they're adults. Why couldn't future computers eventually do the same?

But wait—doesn't that imply a machine that thinks? Isn't the very idea absurd?

The Information Automaton

Computers confuse us because they're both like and unlike other tools—screwdrivers and lawn mowers, television sets and airplanes, mousetraps and microwave ovens. Until recently, these were our entire experience of things mechanical.

All those machines work in stereotyped ways—you've seen one mousetrap, you've seen them all. Bacteria, kittens, and people, however, sense, act, and react in complex, dynamic ways. They have some form of memory, and their behavior can change even without external prompting. They usually act to preserve their existence. Poke them and they poke back. (Or they run.) They're alive. It doesn't much matter what those living things look like. What matters is that their behavior is complex, reactive, and perhaps purposeful. That's what distinguishes them from "mere" machines. No two kittens are the same because no two kittens behave the same. But where does the computer fit? Is it like a jackhammer or like a kitten?

Before computers, machines could do only trivial and repetitive things. They couldn't remember their past, sense their environment, plan their movements, or act and react in complex, dynamic ways. But when they're running big, complex programs, today's computers can do all those things—though still not anywhere as well as even a mouse can. Computers help us do things that until recently required other people's help: editing books, playing games, controlling missiles. With the right software, computers can do mindlike things, although that only intensifies our confusion, because that mindlikeness doesn't extend to everything they do.

They further confuse us because today they're made of metal and plastic, like stereos and lawn mowers, and we can buy them in a store, like ovens and telephones. Most of them don't have arms or legs, they don't eat or breathe or cry (or reproduce), and none of them think for themselves. So we put them in the same class as toasters, cars, and hammers, even though they don't really belong there.

It takes us a long while to see that a new thing is important enough to have its own name. For example, the first modern typewriter was invented in 1867, and the word *typewriter* entered the language a year later. It meant both the machine and the person operating it. We didn't invent the word *typist* until 1885—eighteen years after the typewriter's invention. Similarly, after fifty years of experience with computers, we've finally gotten around to noticing that they have nothing to do with computation, except that we first used them to manipulate numbers. They can also manipulate paintings, prose, poems, or telephone conversations. It's all information. So calling such a device a "computer" is like calling a radio a "wireless telegraph," or a car a "horseless carriage"—which is what we called radios and cars until we got used to the idea that communication has nothing to do with wires and transportation has nothing to do with horses. (Of course, our cars still have horsepower under their hoods.) The problem with calling a computer a machine is this: We don't yet have a word between *mechanical* and *human*. Never before have we had to distinguish between tasks machines can do and tasks only we can do.

Yet how can something be a machine if we can't predict exactly what it will do next? Can something be a machine if it's so complex that its behavior needs a hundred encyclopedias to describe it? Can something be a machine if its behavior changes from hour to hour? The vast array of computer programs running the world's telephone system today already total hundreds of millions of lines of computer instructions and have all three of these attributes. So our telephone system may already be too complex to be accurately described as a "machine." But it isn't human, either.

Computers are now doubling in complexity every eighteen months. Twenty years from now it probably won't make much sense to call these devices "machines." Even if it isn't purposeful or self-aware, it's hard to call something a machine if its behavior is so complex, reactive, and apparently purposeful that it behaves more like a cat than a toaster. Those future computers will force us to make deep changes in the way we look at ourselves and our world. They will force us to look at the universe not as human and nonhuman, living and nonliving, organic and inorganic, but as adaptive and nonadaptive, organized and unorganized, complex and simple. Their very existence will tell us that it's the adaptability, organization, and complexity of living things that make them what they are, not whether they happen to be built of organic molecules.

As computers grow in power and complexity over the next fifty years, the difference between them and, at least, the simpler animals will begin to blur, then disappear. For computers really are akin to animals—rudimentary for the moment, yes, but alike in many ways. Ultimately, it's behavior that matters, not form.

That similarity will, in turn, raise deep questions for us: questions we've never had to ask in quite the same way. Can we really know something if we can't fully articulate it to a computer? Can everything be known in principle and thus reduced to some decision-making process a computer can follow? If not, could computers be made to work anyway? If so, would we understand them? If they become complex enough, would they be alive? If so, would destroying one be like killing a horse? Many disturbing questions—strange and new.

Consequences

What matters it how far we go?
His scaly friend replied,
There is another shore, you know,
Upon the other side.
Lewis Carroll, *Alice's Adventures in Wonderland*

For most of us up to the late nineteenth century, life, in Hobbes' phrase, was nasty, brutish, and short. Real change came only with the industrial revolution. That changed everything. And it started with just one device—the steam engine.

Then, in the 1940s, terrified by new and mysterious weapons and defenses—radar, chemical warfare, submarines, jets, tanks, automated decryption, ballistic missiles, nuclear weapons—all major governments began crash programs to force-feed scientific research.

Today, only two centuries after the start of the industrial revolution, things are about to change again, perhaps more radically, and certainly much more briskly. Why?

First, the surplus food produced by the industrial revolution exploded our population, as the world wars exploded our scientific research. In 1910, there were perhaps twenty thousand scientists; today, there are over five million—one million of them in America alone. Thanks to our enormous population explosion and our subsequent hunger for military and commercial advantage, over 90 percent of all the scientists, engineers, and inventors that have ever lived are still alive. They're all out there right now, inventing materials, machines, weapons, drugs, genes—ideas.

Second, computers, plus increased population and research, have forced a sharp fall in the cost of thinking for the first time since the invention of printing five centuries ago. The number of scientific papers now doubles every decade, and the number of scientists is doubling every two decades. Today, it's easier than ever before to invent, design, and build new devices. Today's Babbages and Turings don't need as much money, expertise, or time. And, because there are far more of them around, new inventions are less likely to be stifled until we become comfortable with them.

Third, computers, population, and research together have exploded the means of communication and transportation. As the price of thinking plummeted, so too did the price of communicating the results of that thinking. Today more people meet and talk to more people and see more connections between more things. Because of faster and more extensive communications, more new things with more new functions are invented by more new people for more new tasks, and all are introduced into society more quickly and more cheaply than ever before.

These accelerators, then, continue to work together to increase population, invention, communication, and automation. Today, the only thing not exploding is our ability to deal with everything that is. We're in a fireball of change.

Unfortunately, it takes us a long time to emotionally digest a new idea. The computer is too big a step, and too recently made, for us to quickly recover our balance and gauge its potential. It's an enormous accelerator, perhaps the greatest one since the plow, twelve thousand years ago. As an intelligence amplifier, it speeds up everything—including itself—and it continually improves because its heart is information or, more plainly, ideas. We can no more calculate its consequences than Babbage could have foreseen antibiotics, the Pill, or space stations.

Further, the effects of those ideas are rapidly compounding, because a computer design is itself just a set of ideas. As we get better at manipulating ideas by building ever better computers, we get better at building even better computers—it's an ever-escalating upward spiral. The early nineteenth century, when the computer's story began, is already so far back that it may as well be the Stone Age.

Today, our fastest, most complex computer, armed with our most sophisticated software, is about as complex as a flatworm. Yet, with its explosive self-improvement, how long will it take for the flatworm to become a fish? If we can teach it to adapt on its own, how long will it be before it becomes as complex as we are? Then more complex still? If it's changing us so much now, what will happen to us then? Today the computer is a blind, deaf, mute, unfeeling flatworm. One day, though, perhaps sooner than you think, it may walk among us. It will be more alien than anything we can ever imagine.

So what will our future be? Wonderful and terrifying.

2

The Greed for Speed

Listen to the technology and find out what it is telling you.
Carver Mead

The common sand that you tread underfoot, let it be cast into the furnace to boil and melt and it will become a crystal as splendid as that through which Galileo and Newton discovered the stars.
Victor Hugo, *Les Misérables*

We carry within us the wonders we seek without us.
Thomas Browne, *Religio Medici*

How do we build computers? Suppose you've just bought a portable computer. It's about as big as a coffee table book, and twice as heavy. It's half the size of Gutenberg's first Bible—and perhaps as important. It may hinge open, like opening a book in the middle; or it may be all one piece, like a tablet. It has almost no moving parts. It has a flat color screen. It may have a keyboard or it may let you use a pen, or both. It has enough temporary memory to hold several dozen novels' worth of information—taking a novel as about half a million letters and punctuation marks. It may have enough permanent memory to hold up to a few thousand novels (about twenty bookcases' worth).

It appears inactive, but in fact it senses its environment in a primitive way through tiny switches hidden in its keyboard, camera, microphone, and other devices. It affects its environment, too, in a simple way, with tiny magnets, lights, and motors hidden in screens, printers, speakers, and other components.

It can add about two hundred million numbers a second but needs less electricity than a light bulb. Soon it will use less energy than a television remote control and will be able to add a thousand million numbers a second. Ten years ago it would have been one of the world's fastest computers; ten years from now it will be a museum piece.

It's still a bit pricey—it costs a few thousand dollars. But within twelve months its price will halve. It will be replaced by an entirely new product line in four months and be obsolete in eight. Early in the next century our technology will have advanced so much that we'll think of our 1990s portable as a piece of useless Victoriana—like a steam-powered paper clip. How is all of that possible?

It's all thanks to one device—the switch—which is very similar to the switches controlling our lights, toasters, and coffeemakers. These switches, however, are far smaller, cheaper, and, above all, far faster. They switch electrons.

Life with the Shape-Shifters

Suppose we've just put the kettle on to boil. For the first few seconds it just sits there, apparently not changing at all. But as the water heats up we eventually notice changes. The kettle grows warm to the touch, we see steam rising from its spout, and we hear water bubbling. We can detect many changes in our environment; if we couldn't, we wouldn't know when to turn off the kettle.

Like all living things, our body is filled with tiny switches—things that change shape as our body and our environment change. We see, hear, smell, taste, and touch with molecular shape-changers that change as the outside world does. We hear a loud noise and the vibration-sensitive switches in our ears change shape; a light flashes and the light-sensitive switches in our eyes change shape. Our nerves detect these molecular shape changes and alert the rest of the body. All these internal changes tell us what is happening in the external world so that our nervous system can use still more internal switches to make sense of these changes. Without the shape-shifters inside us we couldn't even make tea.

A switch is anything that can change *state*—a bicycle pump, a smoke detector, a water valve, a railway shunt. Every switch has to have two or more states. For instance, some of the light-sensitive molecules in our eyes—*rhodopsin* molecules—have at least two possible shapes: one when they're exposed to light and another when they're not. Each shape is a different state. So to build an information manipulator, we're first going to need state changers, lots of them.

A mousetrap has two states: cocked and sprung. A coffeemaker has at least three: off, heating, and brewing. A useful information manipulator needs many more. Today's computers mostly rely on two-state switches; but by linking them together we can make many more states. Each new switch multiplies the number of states the set of switches can have. Thus, each new on-off switch doubles the number of possible states. For instance, you can switch on your toaster, or you can switch on your television set; each separately has only two states, but taken together they have four states: toaster on, television on; toaster on, television off; toaster off, television on; toaster off, television off.

State doubling sounds pretty harmless when it's only done once; but if something doubles in a day, in a week it's over a hundred times bigger, and in a month it's over a thousand million times bigger. So, for example, if a water lily could double its area every day, in less than two months it would cover the earth. Similarly, one two-state switch has two states, but ten such switches connected together have over a thousand states. And a hundred have over a million million million million million states. (Which is rather a lot, because a pile of that many dollar bills would have a mass of more than 180 times that of the earth.) And fewer than four hundred two-state switches have more states than there are atoms in the entire universe.

So a machine with a few million million two-state switches (roughly the capacity of our brain) should have enough states to start doing something really useful. Just writing down the number of possible states would take more digits than there are letters in over 330 bookcases' worth of novels—over a kilometer of shelf space. Don't even ask how much a pile of dollars this big would weigh.

Sense and Sensibility

Every information manipulator needs states, but it also needs some way to sense and affect its environment. Brains are useless without bodies to put them in. For example, think of Goldilocks in the three bears' house. No matter how many states her brain could be in, she couldn't possibly solve her problems without some way to notice her environment—benches, bowls of porridge, beds—and some way to affect her environment—sit on benches, taste porridge, lie on beds, and so on.

So to build an information manipulator we have to make it sense the outside world, just as mousetraps sense mice and toasters sense heat. We also have to make it affect the outside world, just as toasters affect bread and mousetraps affect mice. When we've done so, our information manipulator will be able to sense the world and itself and affect the world and itself, just as Goldilocks sensed, then tested, the bowls of porridge to see which one was at the right temperature. By changing its state our machine is beginning to manipulate information, just as we do, because information is *any difference that makes a difference.* Each change in the world, or in our bodies, informs us of something only if it makes a difference to us. That is, only if it changes our state.

Of course, that state change may occur from internal causes as easily as external ones—our tummy rumbles and we think about having a snack, for example. Yet that state change may not immediately, or ever, lead to behavioral change. If someone tells us it's raining out, for instance, we may make a mental note not to water the lawn tomorrow—then forget—or we may decide to carry an umbrella if we go out—then not go out.

So to manipulate information we need to notice internal or external changes, have a way for those changes to alter our state, and have those state changes possibly alter our behavior. For truly complex behavior, however, we need one thing more, something you're using right now to make sense of this sentence. We need memory.

Remembrance of Things Past

All bacteria have lots of internal switches and lots of ways of noticing and affecting their environment. Yet most of us don't consider them especially interesting, because their behavior is limited—because they lack long-term memory.

Some kinds of bacteria, for example, can swim either in circles or in straight lines. If one of them meets an edible molecule it's more likely to swim in circles for a while. So finding food switches it from moving on to hanging around. Which is a good idea, because if there's one snack here, maybe there are more yummy snacks nearby. Of course, the bacterium doesn't think that. It has no brain to think with. Still, meeting a food morsel altered its state, which in turn altered its behavior. Besides nutrition, the snack also gave it information and so made a difference in its state. Until its hanging-around behavior changes, it "remembers" that it recently encountered food nearby.

The problem with this kind of memory is that it decays quickly. Bacteria can't remember where they last found food after they've wandered away from it. So state-memory is only short-term memory; after a long enough time, it is completely lost.

Recall Goldilocks again. Like that bacterium, she went through the same sense-world-and-change-state cycle in the three bears' house: Is this bed okay? No, too hard. Is this one? No, too soft. How about this one? Yes, just right. However, if there were more uncomfortable beds than her brain had states, after trying enough beds, her brain would eventually run out of new states to be in and would return to some old state. Like a bacterium losing contact with its food source, she would eventually forget which beds she had already tested.

So besides states, an information manipulator needs permanent memory: some way to write down the information it notices. How it does that isn't important. It can be anything from changing the polarity of a magnet to changing the chemical concentration of a cell. What's important is that the memory be as big as it needs to be. Then, armed with permanent memory, our machine could notice that it's been in a certain state before and perhaps do something new: it could ask, "What did I do last time?" and compare its effects in each case. Then it could start noticing patterns—and that's the beginning of everything.

In sum, to build an information manipulator we first need lots of state changers. Linking them so that the state of one affects the state of others results in many states. Linking some of those states to physical effects in the outside world provides a way to sense and affect the world. Finally, by adding long-term memory, we make a device that can recognize, compare, modify, remember, and act on information. Providing we can design it, we now have an information manipulator, whether it's an armadillo, a computer—or us.

The Art of Willful Ignorance

Knowing what goes into an information manipulator is one thing, but knowing how to design one is something else again. With very many switches, sensors, and so on, the complexity of the design task quickly surpasses anything we can hold in our heads at one time. To understand what computer designers do next, let's step back about two centuries to see how another designer understood the inner workings of another complex system—the economy.

While the American Revolution was in full swing in 1776, an absent-minded Scottish moral philosopher named Adam Smith published a run-away bestseller that would become the heart of the future republic's constitution, its political subdivisions, and its manufacturing strength. Here's what he had to say in his *Wealth of Nations* about making pins at a pin factory:

One man draws out the wire, another straights it, a third cuts it, a fourth points it, a fifth grinds it at the top for receiving the head; to make the head requires two or three distinct operations; to put it on is a peculiar business, to whiten the pins is another; it is even a trade by itself to put it into the paper.

Of course, Smith didn't invent the division of labor. That goes back at least to the dawn of humanity when humans were hunters and gatherers. Later, in Greece (almost 2,400 years ago) Xenophon wrote about the cooks in a large household: "Each has his special task, one boiling the meat, another roasting it, one doing the fish in spiced sauce, another frying it, and another making the bread."

Smith's special point was that dividing the task lets each pinmaker produce 4,800 pins a day. Working alone, a pinmaker could make only twenty pins daily. On the other hand, although individual pinmakers can make far fewer pins, each one understands the whole pinmaking process. After the task is minutely divided, however, each worker knows next to nothing about pinmaking. In other words, dividing labor multiplies ignorance.

Luckily, even willful ignorance has a good side. For example, on traditional assembly lines, we have only to do our jobs as well as possible, leaving subsequent stages to the next stations in line. How others do their particular tasks doesn't affect how we work. As long as they do the right thing, that's good enough for us. Simplifying by reduction lets us build very complex things.

Particularly in building computers, it turns out that if we can merely add and test numbers, we can do any numerical operation at all, including complex things like finding square roots. For instance, to subtract one number from another we could first test to see which is smaller, then repeatedly add one to the smaller number and test each time until we get to the larger number. The number of times we have to add one would then be the difference between the two numbers. So to obtain an information manipulator that could solve all arithmetic problems, we can just build a machine that can add and test.

Once we figure out how to add two numbers by using state changers, we can put the whole arrangement of state changers into a box and label it "adder." Similarly, once we know how to determine whether one number is bigger than another, we can put that whole mess into another box and label it "tester." Now whenever we need to add or test, we just reach for a copy of the appropriate box.

Then, once we puzzle out how to subtract, using as many copies of our add and test boxes as we need, we can stick all those boxes in a bigger box and label it "subtracter." We can also create multipliers and dividers from adders, subtracters, and testers. And so it goes. The more complex the function, the bigger the box and the more parts it contains. Yet each new function, no matter how complex, is always being accomplished with only a few kinds of parts.

We can repeat this simplify-then-complexify process as often as we want, thereby building more and more complex things. We do the same thing when we start with letters and make words, then clauses, sentences, paragraphs, sections, chapters, books, bookcases, libraries. Unlike letters in libraries, however, the smallest components of even the world's largest computers are made out of the simplest possible parts—tiny pieces of fused sand.

Faster and Faster

Today's computer chips are made mostly out of melted sand. Being able to make computers mainly out of dirt guarantees that their price will continue to drop a lot for at least the next two decades. Further, today's electronic state changers are not only cheap and plentiful, they're also very small. We can put a million of them on the head of a pin. By early in the next century, we'll be able to put a million of them on the tip of a pin. Finally, not only are they cheap, plentiful, and small, they're also very fast. Some of them can already change state at speeds exceeding four hundred million times a second. They're the fastest things we've ever made.

Because of these four characteristics, the pace of technological change in chip manufacture is simply insane. Now that the computer industry knows how to breathe computational life into dirt, its watchwords have become: smaller, lighter, cheaper, and faster—above all, faster. Consequently, in ten years the power equivalents of today's most advanced computers will be as simple as toasters; in twenty years they'll be as common as pens; and in thirty years they'll be as cheap as paper clips. So squirreling away today's costliest supercomputer to use in ten years would be like saving a snowball in your refrigerator to throw next winter.

Today, one computer chip can have over a hundred million parts. By early in the next century, entire computers may be the size of sugar cubes. Imagine a world filled with millions upon millions of such tiny machines—each equal to a city full of today's primitive computers; each with millions upon millions of parts; each eventually costing only a few cents to make—and each making decisions that will change our world.

An electrical current is really just a river of electrons, and each one of the millions of tiny decision-making boxes inside a computer chip is like a sluice gate controlling whether electrons will flow through it. So a computer chip is a giant electron irrigation project laid out on a nearly flat plane, with microscopic hydroelectric plants, wells, water tanks, and pumps, and millions of canals and sluice gates—enormous complexity working at enormous speeds and tucked into an enormously small space.

In this realm of the fast and the small, a minute is a lifetime and a thumbnail is more real estate than London and Manhattan combined. Here an atom is something we can see and a hundred misplaced atoms is a fatal defect. Watching a chip work, we seem to hear the lilt of a soaring dream. It's the twentieth-century's mandala, an icon of our struggle to achieve order over chaos, an image of our world written in sand with crystalline grace, intricate and beautiful: information made touchable.

All Together Now

Computers are well shaped for what they do, but they will soon be much better. Today's computers are fast, for example, but they aren't as fast as they could be. Half the time a computer is on, it's actually off. Most computers work to the beat of a clock, just as Roman galleys rowed to the beat of a drum. Squads of information quickmarch in lockstep through a computer just as stolidly as those rowing slaves.

Worse yet, most parts of a computer sit idle most of the time. To do anything useful, information has to move into the processor—the place where computers actually compute. So today's computer spends most of its time fighting back tears of boredom, waiting for its processor to do each tiny job and then shuffle tiny pieces of information around for it to do its next tiny job. It's all an immense waste of resources—about as bad as if the world's telephone system could handle only one call at a time.

Today's computer works in that strange way because the first computers worked that way. Back in the 1940s, when modern computers were first designed, electrical wire was fast and cheap, computer processors were fast but costly, and computer memory was both slow and costly. So we designed the computer to shunt information piecemeal into its single expensive processor, then back out to its tiny and expensive memory, using masses of what was then cheap and fast electrical wire.

In those days, a computer was like a high-powered scientist (its processor) locked in a room with many pencils and erasers (its wires) but only one tiny scrap of paper (its memory). Today, however, processors and memory have literally become as cheap as dirt. Consequently, wire is slow and expensive: it takes too long to send information down it, and the more wire we use the fewer processors we have space for.

If we could find a way to share a computer's work between two processors, we would almost double the computer's speed. Computers with several thousand processors working together could be hundreds of times faster than today's single-processor machines. They could be sturdier, too. If anything goes wrong with the single processor in most of today's computers, the whole computer is kaput. A single flawed processor, however, means little if it's just one of thousands.

Yet, although we've had multiprocessor computers since 1981, we still don't know how to divide every problem into a thousand independent pieces so that we can solve it a thousand times faster. For example, how could a thousand washing machines do our laundry a thousand times faster? We can't rinse before we wash, and we can't dry before we rinse. A thousand parents can't make a baby any faster than one set can. Like laundry and childbirth, some processes seem to need a single sequence of steps, none of which we can do before doing all the preceding steps—though that belief may turn out to be illusion. For instance, if we had disposable clothes, the laundry problem would disappear (to be replaced by the disposal problem). So, despite their current problems, there still may be ways to use multiprocessor computers efficiently in every situation. We don't know yet.

If processor and memory costs continue to plummet, however, in ten years personal computers may have scores of processors, each with massive memories. In twenty years, personal computers may become dense sheets or small cubes of millions of tiny computers, like grains of sand on a beach. Such computers may well be cheaper than the electricity used to run them.

Through Yonder Window Breaks

Multiprocessor computers will vastly improve computer speeds, but even they may not be fast enough and cheap enough to solve all our problems. Building computers out of sand lets us almost arbitrarily reduce the energy needed to change state, so our state changers can get ever smaller, cheaper, and faster. That's why the computer industry moves so incredibly quickly. One day, though, we'll look back on that whole technology and think it quaint. Because in the far future—which in the computer world means one or two decades—we may make computers from light beams. Sounds like science fiction, doesn't it? Well, in 1990 AT&T Bell Laboratories built one.

In these optical computers, signals move at the speed of light—about a hundred times faster than those in today's fastest electronic computer. Optical computers using laser beams can also be much more complex than electronic ones, because they can change their internal connections a thousand times a second simply by switching the targets of their laser beams. And, unlike conducting wire, laser beams can cross without interference. Imagine, for example, what would happen to London's incredible traffic snarl if cars could pass right through each other.

With perhaps no moving parts at all, such optical computers may be smaller, lighter, faster, more complex, more densely connected, and nearly indestructible. Of course, to succeed against a mature technology with an enormous investment behind it, every new technology has to be at least ten times better (cheaper, faster, or whatever). We've already invested a great deal in today's computer technology, so optical computers will probably first be hybrids of the two kinds. Further, optical computers haven't yet gone through the manufacturing cycle, so they may be bigger or pricier than electronic computers for a long time. We don't know yet.

Still, it would be only fitting for them to succeed today's silicon-based computers. After all, glass is mostly silicon dioxide, and silicon itself can produce lasers. So an optical computer could be an information manipulator made, once again, of the most common materials on earth—air and dirt.

The Farseeing Eye

Even optical computers may be too slow for some problems, like recognizing faces or understanding speech. To solve those problems we may have to turn to another class of devices entirely: analog machines.

An analog device works by analogy to some physical process. It manipulates some continuously varying physical effect that is roughly analogous to a process we want to model. The movement of a sundial's shadow, for instance, parallels the sun's movement across the sky. An old-fashioned watch keeps pace with that movement by translating the unwinding of a precisely wound watch spring. Similarly, the mercury in a thermometer expands up the tube as its surroundings heat up.

We can make information manipulators work in much the same way, using electronics instead of watch springs or glass and mercury. In modeling a nerve cell, for instance, the flow of electricity in silicon is very like the flow of ions in the cell. Some circuit components can then stand for the cellular equivalent of things like ion pumps, dams, valves, and so on. Building a circuit with those components connected in the right way gives us an analog machine that directly models the nerve cell. Such a device can then function much as a nerve cell does.

A shift to analog machines can greatly speed up some computations. Our eyes, for example, rely partly on analog computations to make sense, rapidly and reliably, of images—whether the images are moving fast or slow or whether it's noon or midnight. They detect the motion of a distant falcon lazily circling in an empty sky or of a particular face out of hundreds at rush hour. They take mountains of messy information and, nearly instantly, see a puppy, a rock, or a building, regardless of whether the body they inhabit is sitting at home, in a moving car, or on a roller-coaster. Old-fashioned computers couldn't even come close to these feats.

By the 1980s, however, biologists had learned enough about how our retina works for chip designers to start building analog chips mimicking some of its operations. These new chips respond directly to light and adapt to huge variations in light levels, as we do. They see things as they happen, notice changes rather than absolute values, track motion, and work even when damaged—all as we do. Some even see optical illusions the way we do. A single cheap chip does all that—without supercomputer backing, intricate programming, or delicate handling.

Of course, these chips can't do everything our highly evolved eyes do, but they do suggest that one day we may be able to build eyes even better than our biological ones. Perhaps they will let us see outside the visible spectrum, see behind our head, zoom in, overlay, annotate, replay, and enhance images. With such eyes, night becomes day, telescopes become irrelevant, and memory becomes perfect.

The computers these eyes are attached to may be just as flexible; because if we can build better artificial eyes, we can also build better computers by using the same principles. Further, as flexibility and reliability increase, huge cheap chips become possible. One such chip could hold hundreds of processors, each with massive memories. These chips would be sturdier, too; they could continue to manipulate information even when they are badly damaged. Unlike today's fragile computers, they would no longer be destroyed by dust specks.

Biodegradable Machines

Today's computers are small, but they could become much smaller. If we look far enough into our own bodies, we see that everything turns on information, machines, and factories. Almost all the hundred million million cells in each of us carry a copy of about eight bookcases' worth of how-to books. Millions upon millions of cellular machines in our cells use that archive to make still more cellular machines. Out of that sea of mindless activity comes life.

Today, we're trying to build biological computers out of that same sea. Such computers would use the same cell chemistry our body does. Today we often refer to a computer crash by saying that the computer has died; in the far future, we may have to use the phrase literally.

We have already built touch, smell, and taste sensors with biological materials. We also have memory devices made of light-sensitive molecules extracted from vats of bacteria. Primitive devices have been built by using brain cells extracted from rats, and some of them grow nerve cells in precise configurations directly on computer chips. Eventually, we might be able to build whole computers that way. Imagine buying a computer made out of rat brains.

We probably won't build them anytime soon though. They may need high-priced life-support systems. Or they may get sick too easily. Perhaps they will not live long enough to be useful. Who knows? But one day, what we call a *computer* may be something grown in a vat that will clamber out clothed in flesh. And a *computer virus* may be something that we too can catch.

In our quest for ever more speed we may eventually fuse computers and biology into a single new technology by engineering molecular machines. That development took a long step forward in 1981, when two IBM scientists made a microscope that let us see and move single atoms. Five years later they got the Nobel Prize. Similar microscopes are now teacup-sized and available commercially. Then, in 1990, IBM took hours and used a massive cooling system to write the letters I–B–M using single atoms. Less than a year later, Hitachi could do similar things—but in seconds, and at room temperature. By 1992, researchers were building conducting wires one molecule thick. By 1995, others were building simple motors almost the size of molecules. By 1996, yet others were connecting those motors together.

By early in the next century, we may be building simple molecular machines an atom at a time. Of course, it's a long step from that to building cheap molecular computers, but the technology is moving incredibly fast—much faster even than electronic technology. Also, we know it's possible, because such molecular machines fill our very bodies. They are what we are and how we work.

Molecular computers could be millions of times more energy efficient than today's computers and work a million times faster. And they could be a hundred million times smaller. To solve a problem we wouldn't so much program a computer, as we do today, but grow one. In forty years, something bee-sized may carry more memory and computing power than all today's computers put together. It might even look a lot like a bee.

The Solid State

It's 1997 and you've just bought a computer. What kind of computer could you buy in 2021 for the same money? Assuming computer performance keeps doubling for the same price every year and a half, by 2021 for the same money you could buy a machine costing $131 million in 1997 dollars. Today, such a machine would be powerful enough to handle all North America's present aviation control systems, or juggle all the variables in a world-spanning military wargame. By 2021 all that power could be in a bangle on your wrist. And, for the same money, by 2045 you could have $8500 million 1997 dollars worth of machine— four times the power of the entire world's supply of supercomputers in 1997—all in your designer sunglasses.

All this change in computer technology will have consequences for all of us. It's already true that in today's computer hardware world, yesterday's technological miracle is tomorrow's obsolete junk. But that progress has a cost. Each leap forward has also meant a leap in complexity, and each leap in complexity has meant a further loss of understanding.

Here's why. Under a microscope, today's computer chips look like well-designed cities. If we take each chip component as a city block, in the early 1970s a typical chip would have covered a city twenty-two kilometers across. By the end of that decade, it would have covered Chicago. By the late 1980s, it would have covered Texas. Today, it would cover half the earth's land surface. And, by century's end, it would cover the earth—oceans included. A decade or so after that it would cover all the planets.

Every time the density of the chips has leapt up, so has their complexity. The number of state changers on a single chip is now rapidly approaching a thousand million—roughly the complexity of a worm's brain. Unlike a worm's brain, however, that number is continuing to double every eighteen months. Computer complexity will inevitably exceed the limits of anything we can truly understand. Perhaps quite soon too.

Of course, there are financial and physical limits on how far we can improve today's computers. For example, every halving of chip size quadruples the cost. Further, because every state changer generates some waste heat, if we make the computer too dense, it won't compute—it will melt. So, to avoid that, we must separate its parts more, making it slower—the wider the circuit separation, the longer the communication delay.

Thus, there's a certain size and speed beyond which we can't build computers with normal materials. For instance, no molecular computer could be as big as a cubic meter; it would radiate a terawatt a second—

about five times as much energy as the entire United States now uses in the same period. (Besides doing all the world's computing, it could double as a miniature sun.) We may surmount even these problems with even more-esoteric devices now on the drawing board, like condensed-matter computers, superconducting computers, or quantum computers. Still, it will take major new engineering to make such devices work. For the next two decades or so, we'll probably stay within the limits of present-day technology, which can still produce computers up to a hundred million times better than they are today. There's plenty of room to grow.

Up the Future's Endless Stair

Linguists have a saying: The map isn't the territory. They mean that the word *cow*, for instance, isn't a cow. The word *cow* can't give milk, nor can it moo. Similarly, as the Belgian painter René Magritte showed, a painting of a pipe is only a painting, and not a pipe. What's true for most things, however, almost isn't true for computers.

Before we even build a computer, the mere diagram of its circuits, together with information about their timings, heat dissipation, and noise immunity, almost is a computer. We can simulate the whole thing—and during design we often do—on a slower, simpler computer. Manufacturing it only makes it cheaper, faster, and more widely available.

So a mere design of a computer is itself almost a computer, which makes computers vastly different from other tools. If we simulate a bridge, say, it can't carry real traffic—only simulated traffic—whereas a simulated computer is just as real and just as useful as a physical one. In other words, unlike almost every other physical artifact we know, computers depend mainly on the arrangement of their parts, not on the parts themselves. Computer design is more like book writing than it is like house building; the fonts we use don't matter as much as the bricks we use. That's why we can so easily make computers smaller, faster, and cheaper simply by replacing one set of parts with another smaller, faster, cheaper set. And, as the parts get smaller and cheaper, more diverse and more numerous, the design problem becomes less one of how to build the parts, and more one of how to arrange them to do their job.

So, besides solving various physical problems—avoiding manufacturing defects, venting waste heat, and reducing communication delays—the biggest obstacle to producing more complex computers today is sheer design complexity. A light airplane has around five thousand parts; a jumbo jet has about three million; and a space shuttle has six million. Some of today's computers already have a *thousand* times that many parts. They're unthinkably complex, and they're getting more unthinkably complex all the time.

Consequently, even armed with massive computer programs to handle most of the design details, it still takes several dozen highly trained (and very expensive) people a year and a half to two years to design a new chip. The chips themselves take only a few weeks or months to make. So without some radical change, design complexity will be the next big bottleneck to our endless, insatiable, relentless demand for more speed.

Today, computers do all the design grunt work and control most of the delicate fabrication to make the next generation of computers. As they get cheaper and more powerful, they help us design their next generation's ever-cheaper and yet-more-powerful computers. And the more complex they get, the less we understand them. Each year, the decisions we make about their design are moved further and further back from the ways they are implemented, and the connections between those high-level decisions and the resulting computers grow ever more tenuous. Consequently, to keep on the spiral of increased complexity we're going to have to hand over more and yet more of the decisions about their own design to them.

Already, computers make computers; they're quickly shoving us out of their almost fully automated and almost totally dust-free factories. We're becoming brood hens, more and more puzzled by the curious eggs we keep laying. Eventually, none of us may know exactly what's in any computer. Year by year, we're rapidly gaining power and, just as rapidly, losing control. There's only one other similar process in all our experience—a thermonuclear explosion.

Expecting Company

You can tell how many seeds are in the apple, but not how many apples are in the seed.

Ken Kesey

Just as today's computers have electronic switches that change state, so our brain has nerve cells—something like a hundred thousand million of them—that change state. Today, about ten thousand chips could hold that many electronic state changers, which are roughly a hundred thousand times smaller and a million times faster than nerve cells. So we could pack a space the size of our brain with chips. That seems to be the future of computers. So why haven't we done it yet? Let's go through the problems, from easy to hard.

First, nerve cells can fire at several hundred different rates, and the nerve cells each of them are attached to can react to those changes and alter their timing and firing rates as well; so each cell has many more states than the simple two states of today's electronic state changers. That's no problem. We can replace a complex state changer with many two-state ones: it will merely be bigger.

Second, nerve cells come in several hundred different types, whereas today's chips carry only a few kinds of state changers. Again, that's no problem. We can design more complicated ones, if necessary.

Third, nerve cells use one-fiftieth the voltage and one ten-millionth the energy of today's electronic state changers. (Guess what?) That's no problem. At the current technological growth rate, we should surmount that obstacle within the next two decades.

Fourth, many nerve cells work at the same time, while most state changers in today's chips do nothing most of the time. That's a problem. We still don't know how to make multiprocessor computers solve every problem efficiently. On the other hand, our brain doesn't do especially well with some problems—like arithmetic—either; so perhaps this isn't a serious drawback. It may not be necessary to be able to solve every single problem efficiently.

Fifth, many nerve cells connect to forty thousand others, and a few connect to perhaps a million others, whereas our most complex chips today connect each state changer to only about ten others. Now, that's a serious problem. To solve it, we'll have to rethink our whole electronic technology and perhaps go to optical or biological computers.

Sixth, and last, even if we could connect many complex, specialized, efficient, and densely connected state changers, we still won't know how to connect them correctly. None of the other problems really matter; we can lick them all in a few decades with enough money. But this one does. We may have to develop molecular computers before we can solve it. Our brain's wiring is a by-product of over two thousand million years of evolution—and it's fiendishly intricate.

To see how intricate, imagine giving each of all six thousand million of us alive today forty thousand telephones. About a thousand times a second forty thousand people call you and leave a (very brief) message on your answering machine. Some encourage and others discourage you from calling other people. You listen to some people more than others and can vary the attention you give to their chatter. Sometimes you even call yourself.

Depending on how many and what kind of calls come in, you might get more and more excited. If you get excited enough, then a hundred times a second or so you call forty thousand others with your own (brief) words of encouragement or discouragement. Or perhaps you call for random reasons—because of a slight overconcentration of sodium or potassium ions nearby, a slight drop in oxygen, a too rhythmic tickling of encouragements from your neighbors. Or perhaps your body has released certain hormones, or has taken a psychoactive substance like coffee, chocolate, aspirin, nicotine, alcohol, psilocybin, or heroin.

You're connected to all the other nerve cells with enough neural wiring to stretch around the world two and a half times. Connected through the wire, you belong to many sewing circles, each excitedly gossiping about the latest thing that just happened. Depending on the circle, it could be that someone connected to the outside world noticed something moving. Or perhaps another circle's activity triggered an old memory. Or perhaps the rhythm of activity in one of your own circles triggered a tiny muscle spasm, which triggered another circle, and so on.

That intricate dance of excitations goes on all day and all night, even during sleep. But which nerve cells connect to which others, and exactly how do they relate to brain function? We don't know. We may never know. We have a rough idea for some parts of the brain—like the vision and hearing centers—so for those parts we've already built something similar into computers. But it will probably be two or three more decades before we can build anything approaching our brain's enormous complexity. And until we learn how to connect its parts together, it won't do anything as spectacular as what we can do with the merest thought.

Each of us carries around the most complex thinking machine on the planet. But listen to the technology: It's complexity and organization that matter, not cells versus chips. Computers forty years from now may well become at least as complex as we are, and anything that complicated won't be understandable. Eventually it won't even be controllable. All parents know that.

So perhaps we should use these wonderful brains of ours to start planning for company. Because when it comes we won't understand it. And soon after that, we won't control it either.

3

Precisely Speaking

When we say, for instance, that Napoleon ordered armies to go to war we combine in one single expression a series of consecutive commands dependent one on another.

Leo Tolstoy, *War and Peace*, epilogue

Fortran's tragic fate has been its wide acceptance, mentally chaining thousands and thousands of programmers to our past mistakes.

Edsger Dijkstra, *The Humble Programmer*

The limits of my language mean the limits of my world.

Ludwig Wittgenstein, *Tractatus Logico-Philosophicus*

How do we talk to computers? We can train dogs to fetch sticks and frisbees—though cats, of course, sensibly ignore us—but how could we possibly get a mere machine to understand what we say?

Tolstoy gives us a hint in his epilogue to *War and Peace:*

Napoleon could not have commanded an invasion of Russia and never did so. One day he ordered certain documents to be dispatched to Vienna, to Berlin and to Petersburg; the following day saw such and such decrees and orders issued to the army, the fleet, the commissariat, and so on and so on—millions of separate commands making up a series of commands corresponding to a series of events which brought the French armies into Russia.

That's precisely what happens when we tell a computer to do something. We issue a command that looks, to us, simple—something like "Invade Russia" or "Add this number to that one." These commands aren't really so simple for the computer though. To obey the second one, for instance, the computer must first find the two numbers we're referring to, decide how to interpret the instruction "add them," and actually do it. Finally, it must decide what to do with the sum: Should it replace the first number, the second, or neither? Once it's done all that, it must turn everything into sequences of even more basic instructions: "If this magnet is polarized one way and that switch is on, then flip this other switch." Only when it has done this can it actually obey our command to add two numbers. And before that, someone must have explained how to do it all, in exact and excruciating detail.

It's no use appealing to the computer's native intelligence. It has none. Even if it had, it would often find it hard to guess our intent. A cook in Napoleon's army, for example, may have had no idea why he was ordered to prepare his cart and victuals. He could safely conclude that he was going to be asked to march somewhere in the next few days, but other than that he was too far down the chain of command to know what to do without being given precise instructions.

Today's computers are good because they do exactly as we say. And they're bad because they do exactly as we say. To work at all, they need a language both they and we understand, even if neither of us understand each other's native tongue. Fortunately, we've had that problem many times before. To solve it we invented pidgins.

The Chinese Had a Word for It

The words *feet, mice, lice, geese, teeth, men,* and *women,* are the only common English plurals internally different from their singulars. Those mutated plurals are holdovers from Old English, the language that survived in England until about the twelfth century. Once, long ago, English had many mutated plurals. Had British history been different, for example, the plurals of *book, oak,* and *goat,* might today be *beek, eak,* and *geat.* Other odd plurals exist—like *oxen* and *children*—but they don't change internally. There are also words whose plurals are the same as their singulars—like *sheep, swine, deer, folk,* and *fish*—though we can still say "You folks, feed the fishes" (or, in what might be a Mafiosi expression, "Sleep with the fishes, you folks").

Like every other human language, English is full of such word fossils, partly because languages change when they collide. When speakers of two language groups meet with no interpreters around, they rapidly make up a paralanguage—a pidgin. Initially the pidgin is very clumsy because it has no native speakers, but children who grow up hearing only the pidgin generalize it, and it quickly slips into a true language.

The work of developing a pidgin often falls to the weaker group— people with butter but no guns (or with guns but no ships, or with ships but no money). Luckily for them, every language has both deep and superficial features. So English-speaking tourists in Brazil, for instance, will often use Portuguese words in English word order—to the endless amusement of Brazilians. Word order, or syntax, is part of the deep structure of many languages, whereas nouns, say, are usually part of the superficial structure. Syntax is hard to change. So it's often easier for a people to create a pidgin by simply replacing some of their own language's more superficial features with those of the other group's language.

That's probably what happened to the Anglo-Saxons, who spoke Old English, in the eighth and ninth centuries when the Vikings, who spoke mostly Old Norse, invaded Britain. The subsequent linguistic disruption (never mind the pillage, rape, and other consequences of invasion) may have helped kill off most of Old English's mutated plurals, leaving only seven diehards today as reminders of vanished times. Of course, linguistic change was old news to the Anglo-Saxons. If they themselves hadn't invaded Britain earlier, English might have become a Romance language, like French or Italian; after all, the Romans had invaded long before. Or, if the Romans hadn't invaded, English might have been a Celtic language, like Welsh or Irish. Similarly, without the Viking invasions, English might have become a Low German language, like Dutch or Flemish. After the Vikings, of course, came the Normans, who spoke a form of French. And so on, down the long, sad centuries.

That linguistic change didn't just occur in Britain. The word *pidgin* is itself derived from a Chinese pronunciation of the word *business*. The Chinese—forced at gunpoint by the British to trade Indian opium and cotton for silver, tea, silks, and porcelain—couldn't pronounce *business*. They produced something like *bijeon*, which eventually turned into *pidgin*. That business resulted in a few hundred very rich British merchants, twelve million Chinese opium addicts, the Opium Wars, and the founding of Hong Kong.

Over the centuries and across the globe, successive waves of invasion or trade forced colliding languages to pidginize. Today, the same thing is happening between us and computers.

A Visit to Paris

Any non-French–speaker seriously thinking about becoming a computer programmer should first visit France—Paris in particular. Nothing better teaches the difficulties of computer programming today than trying to make ourselves understood in a foreign country. Like non-French–speaking tourists in France, we need a translator when we deal with the computer.

In the late 1940s, before we had any kind of computer translator, the equivalent of driving around alone in France (that is, operating a computer) meant stopping every now and then and getting under the car to reconnect wires in the car's entrails. It was slow, hard, and unbelievably annoying work. Getting anywhere at all took forever. Then, around 1950, we got Pierre, a little computer program that stood between us and some of the uglier parts of the computer.

Our instructions to Pierre, our French driver—who obviously thought he was competing in the Grand Prix and, like Boston cab drivers, had *très charmant* notions about road safety—had to be quite precise. They also had to be in French. Pierre's uncompromising refusal to understand English, or, for that matter, any French dialect other than Parisian French, forced us to be clear and exact. Suppose, for instance, we wanted to get to the Champs-Elysées. We couldn't simply tell Pierre and leave the driving to him. We first had to turn our wish into a long sequence of simple commands he could understand. He then turned that enormously detailed set of commands into actions at the steering wheel, accelerator, and brakes. In effect, Pierre wasn't driving the car—we were.

Pierre was definitely a help, but his driving could only be described as reckless. And he was particularly dense. He understood only two words—*yes* and *no*; or rather, since he refused to understand anything but French, *oui* and *non*. At every fork in the road we had to say *oui* or *non*. It was indescribably tedious. It was so tedious that around 1955, when the car grew powerful enough to carry more people, we got Jacqueline, a slightly more advanced translator. Of course, Jacqueline didn't speak English either, but she knew Pierre really well. She understood how to turn more complex commands like "Turn left after the next hospital you see on the right" into long sequences of commands, each one simple enough for even Pierre to understand. Although Jacqueline was an improvement, we still had to say many tedious, repetitive things that were prone to error. If we mistranslated our request to be taken to the Tuileries Gardens as a request to ram the next overtaking vehicle, she cheerfully obliged. Even if we had given her directions to get to the Eiffel Tower thousands of times before, we had to repeat the same specific, detailed instructions each time we wanted to go there. She hadn't the least idea what tourists liked to do in Paris and always greeted our instructions with the same air of astonishment.

So, around 1960, when the car became even more powerful, we obtained an even more advanced translator, François. François was like a rudimentary tourist guide. He knew a little bit about what tourists liked to do and where they liked to go; but best of all, he understood a crude pidgin English. He translated our commands into a long series of simpler commands to Jacqueline, who in turn translated these into an even longer series of even simpler commands to Pierre. Although we were in some sense still driving the car ourselves, we had managed to compress a lot of the immense length of simple instructions into tolerably short sequences of more complex instructions. Finally, we could get around France with something approximating ease (at least when going to well-known destinations). We had invented the idea of computer programming languages.

Words into Deeds

To many of us, the phrase "computer language" is just as contradictory as "military intelligence" or "selfless politician." How could a mere machine possibly understand a language? Without thinking about it too much, we would probably say that a mere machine can't understand anything, far less something as complicated as a language. Still, without getting into philosophical subtleties, it's okay to say that a computer can understand lots of simple things, if we first explain them carefully enough using a small number of well-chosen commands.

For example, suppose Napoleon had had to invade Russia with a very stupid army. Let's say he first orders it to "Invade Russia." This army of idiots, however, doesn't know how to do that, although it has a small set of simple things it *can* do: collect food, wine, prostitutes, carts, horses, and weapons; start marching; stop marching; kill people; and so on. So Napoleon would have to translate his one command, "Invade Russia," into a series of simpler commands, like: "Call the troops together. Start marching to the east. Kill anyone who resists your march." Suppose his troops are so thick that they still don't understand. He would then have to turn even these simple commands into sequences of even simpler ones, until they're at a level his simpleton army can understand. Then, finally, he could have his war.

Fortunately for the art of warfare, if enough leaders of idiot armies had to go through that tedious process, they would probably meet at conferences and compare experiences. They might then see that certain procedures are common to most campaigns and could work out long, detailed sequences of basic instructions explaining universal procedures: How to recognize the enemy, how to despoil the countryside, how to operate in winter, how to wage war at sea, how to loot and rape, and so on.

Next, they could think up statements that let them link those common procedures together to make the performance of some actions dependent on the outcome of others. Like the syntax of human languages, these linking statements would determine how, or if, or when, other statements are interpreted. For example:

While in enemy territory: Find an untouched building. *If* it's a church, *then* loot it; *otherwise*, burn it. *Repeat until* no untouched buildings remain.

To better display the structure, we can write these linking commands the way a contemporary programmer would:

while in enemy territory
   find an untouched building
  if it's a church
    then loot it
    else burn it
until no building is untouched

Armed with those special linking statements to control all the other statements, military leaders could specify any sequence of actions expressible in terms of the few primitive actions their armies already understand. They would have created an army-programming language they could use to explain to any army—no matter how dense its soldiers—how to invade anywhere, anytime.

Unfortunately, they would still have to go through the tedious translation process to turn their high-level commands into sequences of basic instructions their armies could understand. Luckily for them, though, the translation process is *itself* a process, just like looting churches. Although much more complicated, it goes something like this:

Repeat step *a* until *b* happens; then go to step *c*, unless *d* happens; in which case, repeat step *e* five times or as many times as you repeated step *a*, whichever is bigger.

Once their armies are smart enough to at least make simple decisions and follow any sequence of simple instructions, however long, the generals can tell them to follow a sequence of instructions that, together, explain how to follow a sequence of yet-more-complex instructions. Which the generals could then use to explain how to follow any sequence of even more complex instructions. And so on, forever.

In other words, unlike a washing machine or a toaster, a computer is so versatile that it can ingest the product of its own efforts. We can't turn toast into breadmaking instructions; nor can we turn clean shirts into instructions on how to wash curtains. But in the computer, one program can produce another program, which can produce a third, and so on. We can use the computer itself to translate our instructions to it.

Alas—to get back to Napoleon for a moment—Napoleon's translator is merely a complex rule book and not a military genius. It doesn't make it impossible for Napoleon to blunder. For example, while following Napoleon's orders to the letter, some of his brighter soldiers might see an opening in their lines and wish to cover it. But they can't. Perhaps their short but crafty general is leaving the hole to entice the enemy to attack there. So, when the general really does blunder, a Waterloo happens. Like dim-witted but endlessly patient foot soldiers, today's computer languages can't tell the difference between a brilliant sacrifice and a colossal bungle. They obey their every command exactly and without question, trusting that their fearless leaders know what they're doing. Which leads to problems—because their leaders often don't.

Learning from the Past

In the 1940s, 1950s, and early 1960s, computers were costly, cranky, clumsy, and, above all, customized. Because each machine was one-of-a-kind, each program had to be hand-tailored to the particular local machine—which encouraged designers to use lots of tricks and low cunning to squeeze the most performance from the machine—which, in turn, emphasized program efficiency over programmer efficiency.

Since programmers were cheap, plentiful, replaceable, and flexible—but computers weren't—the time programmers took to create programs didn't count for much compared to the time computers took to run the programs. So programmers had to go through great contortions to save the machines even a few seconds. Their programs usually became impossible to understand—even by the same programmer only a few months later. But at least it was fun; and it gave great job security. You can't get fired if nobody understands what you do.

Because the technology changed so rapidly, and because programs depended heavily on each machine's special structure, when a new computer replaced the old one, all the old programs became useless. (Imagine what a tough life appliance makers would have if every electric wall outlet and every town's voltage were different.) As there was almost no way to build on old expertise, programmers—to avoid being further devalued—put even more emphasis on artful dodges and machine-specific tricks. Job security is important, after all.

Moreover, because there was almost no sharing of knowledge among designers of different types of machine, discovering general programming principles took a long time. Not until the late 1960s—two decades after the first modern computers were developed—did anyone even realize that systematic programming was possible. And, because no one could compare machines and programs directly, everyone had to reinvent the wheel again and again. And again.

Those ancient programmers were like a group of farmers isolated by tall mountains. All their farms were different—there were vineyards, dairy farms, chicken ranches, and sugarcane plantations. Even when a few hardy farmers hiked over the mountains to gossip, they had little to say to each other, because their experiences were so different. About all they could talk about was gravity, sunlight, and air pressure. Even when someone invented crop rotation or fertilizer or tractors, it took a long time for that knowledge to trickle over to the others, for they had to find ways to transfer the new idea to their particular domains.

That was the state of programming up to the late 1950s. Luckily, programmers then developed something entirely new; it was as if those isolated farmers had strung telephone lines over the mountains and all switched to, say, potato farming. They could then both talk to each other and have something in common to chat about. The programmers had developed computer pidgins.

The Ladder of Life

Back in the 1950s programmers had nothing tangible to show for all their work—it's hard to quantify ease of use. Of course, every visiting dignitary could see that the machine was an imposing edifice, obviously costing a fortune and needing many minions to guard and protect it. It was clear that to use, never mind understand, the machine you had to be a genius. Still, in those days, even geniuses were easier to find—and simpler to understand—than computers were. Thus was born the superstition that the machine's time and convenience were far more important than ours. We were there to serve, not to control the machine.

You see, the machine was magical. It somehow manipulated information in an age when most other machines were just overgrown power tools. Like kittens playing with our first mirror, we had no idea what it was or what it could do. No one could dispute the technical elite because no one—often including most of the elite themselves—understood the machines. What they did, how they did it, what they could do, these were all mysteries to almost everyone, including the biggest companies and the biggest names in computing today.

As a result, a ladder of relative importance evolved. On the highest rung were the machine builders. As they actually built the machine, they were the source of all the good and important things it could do. However, they built machines that were easy to build, not necessarily easy to use. Next came the machine maintainers. In those days, computers were so flaky we mainly classified them according to their average time between failures—only a few minutes or hours. So maintainers were second in importance only to builders. They imposed whatever duty cycle—and resulting down time—they wanted, without regard for those paying the bills.

Then came the pidgin designers. Because they made it possible to talk to the machine in a sensible way, their concerns took precedence over everyone else's but the hardware folks. Like the builders, they followed their natural inclinations and built pidgins that were easy to build, not necessarily easy to use. Next came the programmers. They created programs in whatever pidgin was in use at their local installation—ostensibly for the machine's users but actually with their own curiosity, convenience, and interests in mind. Again, they built programs that were easy to devise— and, more to the point, easy to sell—but still not necessarily easy to use.

The users, the lowest of the low, were dependent on the machine for economic, technical, or military reasons. They just had to put up with the inconvenience and pay all the bills.

They still do, for the totem pole still exists today: grinning machines at the top and groaning users at the bottom. The first hardware and software designers taught the next generation, who codified the consensus into textbooks, which then shaped succeeding generations, even unto the present day. Today, computer chips are dirt cheap, at least compared to the cost of our time, or the cost of a major programming error in, say, a space shuttle launch or a nuclear weapon test. Yet we're still saddled with the primitive ways of talking to them we invented forty years ago to produce company payrolls or analyze mathematical equations on primeval machines millions of times weaker and simpler than today's.

As happens with all things human, in the fullness of time early decisions made to surmount short-term problems became hallowed by the voice of tradition and superstition into nearly unbreakable commandments. "Don't fix it if it ain't broke" is the usual formula. Thus the totem pole persists.

Living on the Frontier

Computing is still very much a frontier science. The first machines, pidgins, and programs were feats of the imagination. It's amazing that engineers got those crazy-quilt patchworks of cobbled-together systems to work at all. Those engineers had to be rugged individualists, square-jawed, can-do people who always knew—or had to pretend to know—what to do with the new magical mirror. Like religious zealots, they brooked little argument, because any crack in their confidence could bring down the whole edifice. Never ask someone building a castle in the air what's supporting it.

In those days, it took heroic measures to get the machine to work at all. The times required courage, vision, and persistence to face the tremendous challenges. Back then, even the vibration of a passing car or plane could crash the computer. Obviously, in an age when it took a supreme effort just to keep a multimillion-dollar machine working for a few minutes at a time, there was no chance that consumers, or even programmers for that matter, would have any real say.

Each computer was surrounded by the achingly exciting aura of an experimental laboratory. It was hugely expensive and very, very sexy, a one-of-a-kind, once-in-a-lifetime experiment. It was a privilege merely to be allowed to work there. So the emphasis was on research and development, not production. Ideas mattered. People didn't.

Computers were like cyclotrons and nuclear power stations were four decades ago, or space stations are today. We don't require space stations to be immediately profitable or easy to use. If we did, we would never have built the first one. We get around their technical refractoriness by allowing only highly trained and extremely competent people near them. Like space stations, computers have—and had—military, economic, and political consequences, and so a lot of government money was spent on them, particularly in the early days.

Today, computers work for days or weeks at a time without breaking down, but the ease-of-use problem remains. Most computer systems are still rough-and-ready. We'll have to wait until they can keep working for years at a time—like washing machines and toasters—before consumers count for much.

Nor should that surprise us, really. Back in the fifties and sixties it was so hard to do anything at all, or even to foresee what could be done, that we did what's easiest first. What's possible? We had no idea. We still don't. So we did what we could, not necessarily what, in hindsight, might have been best.

That's true in every new field of study because we're always stumbling backward into our future. Like genetic engineering, computer technology is so useful that demand for it grew too strong too early, and the builders started selling it to foolhardy people who absolutely had to have it. Even today, though, it isn't really ready. We have only to look at the sorry state of computer pidgins to see that.

Watching Our Language

A mathematician, a physicist, and an engineer are traveling by train through Scotland when they spot a sheep walking in the same direction that the train is moving.

"Look," says the engineer, jumping up from the seat, "Scottish sheep are black!"

"No," says the physicist tiredly, "You engineers are always going off half-cocked. From the information given, all we can say is that at least one Scottish sheep is black."

"No," says the mathematician, settling back in the seat, "We can but say that there is at least one sheep in Scotland that's black on at least one side."

That's how exact we have to be when we program today, and that's how literally computers follow our commands. Here's an example: In the summer of 1963, a group at the U.S. National Aeronautics and Space Administration was working on mission control computer systems for the upcoming Apollo moon shots. One of the programmers was testing an old orbit-computation program previously used during the suborbital Mercury flights. For weeks he struggled to understand why the answers he got from the program were always a bit off. Finally, he found a statement something like this:

DO 400 I = 1.10

That's a statement in Fortran, the most ancient of computer pidgins. In Fortran dialects, most spaces don't matter, usually only names appear to the left of an equal sign, and names can be almost anything. So the computer, following its rigid translation rule-book, understood the statement as:

DO400I = 1.10

that is, "Put the number 1.10 in the box named DO400I." But what the original programmer actually meant was:

DO 400 I = 1,10

that is, "Repeat ten times the following commands up to the command labeled 400."

So the original programmer intended the computer to do one thing but the computer thought the instruction meant something completely different, all because a period replaced a comma. If that apparently tiny mistake had made it into an Apollo spacecraft, the whole ship, not to mention its crew, could have been lost. A quarter of a million lines of computer instructions, each one just as finicky as that one line, control space shuttle launches today; many millions of such lines run the world's telephone system; and many more millions control nuclear weapons.

We blunder all the time. We don't want machines so stupid that they do exactly what we say, instead of what we so obviously mean. Yet if it's so obvious what we mean, why can't computers catch the error? You might think that after we made enough such mistakes and lost enough high-priced equipment in space—or killed enough people on earth—we could design computer pidgins to make such errors impossible. But you would be wrong.

The Unimportance of Being Earnest

Today's computer pidgins are hard to learn and hard to use. All are cryptic, precise, and dense. That in itself isn't so bad, because millions of normal people have learned a similar language: they've learned how to crochet from a book. Here, for example, are the first few lines of crochet instructions for a linen doily edging of hearts and fans:

Materials: One 350-yard ball of ecru Knit Cro-Sheen or suitable substitute. Size 5 steel crochet hook. 13-inch square of linen fabric.
Gauge: 8 hdc = 1 inch.
Instructions: Make four strips as follows: Ch 99.
Row 1: Sc in 2nd ch from hook and in each ch across. Ch 4, turn.
Row 2: Sk 1st 2 sc, hdc in each of next 2 sc, * ch 2, sk 2 sc, 1 hdc in each of next 2 sc, rep from * to end with sk 2 sc, hdc in turning ch, ch 2, turn.

If you don't crochet, knit, or do cross-stitch, these instructions are probably gibberish to you, but with a little practice and background knowledge, you too could be crocheting away by following the instructions, just as most programmers can read and understand small programs written in a language they know.

Most of today's computer languages are as peculiar as the language of crocheting. Yet even the rankest beginner can learn to crochet a doily or scarf in a few hours, whereas it often takes computer beginners days or weeks before they can program anything interesting. Why? Unlike crocheting, the mountain of detail in most of today's computer pidgins makes it hard for beginners to connect what they're learning with what they want to do. The computer instructions they have to learn are too small scale and too far removed from anything they really want to do. In effect, they're being asked to run corporations by being told how to use paper clips.

Today's pidgins are also a minefield of booby traps. They emphasize making fast programs—and making programming fast—rather than making understandable programs—and making programming understandable. They're designed for an age when computers were priceless, program speed was paramount, programs were tiny, programmers were cheap, and users were irrelevant. Which was fine when we were only crocheting scarves, but not so fine now that we're trying to crochet nuclear power stations.

Science and Psychology

Before we learned about genes, we usually grouped living things by how they looked. For centuries we thought of whales and dolphins as fish because they looked more like fish than such mammals as mice and cows and people. If two things looked different, they were, presumably, fundamentally different. Although we now know that there's almost no genetic difference between one person and another, racism, sexism, and various other -isms haven't gone away. Appearances still matter to us.

Similarly, to a programmer, a program's layout provides important clues to its meaning, just as a book's layout gives readers important clues to its meaning. Today, however, whether programmers indent program lines or they don't, whether they join the lines together or they don't—it's all the same to the computer. Imagine if every book you read consisted of one long, continuous sentence. Why then don't the designers of languages devise ways to let computers interpret layout information like indents and line endings?

A little bit of history may explain why they don't. In the early days of writing in Europe, scribes used abbreviations, ran their words together, and filled up as much of the space on the vellum or parchment as they could. Scribes, after all, were scarce, readers were few, and writing materials were expensive—a few sheets of vellum meant killing a calf. So it was very important to make the most of the space available. With the coming of the printing press, cheap paper, and widespread literacy things changed. The reader's time now became far more expensive than the writing material. So printers started spacing the words, punctuating sentences, expanding abbreviations, and breaking the text into sentences, paragraphs, and chapters. If paper had remained expensive and readers few, none of that would have happened.

Just as ancient scribes strove to reduce their writing space, ancient programmers strove to reduce the time it took to run a program. One consequence of this effort was that they let their computers ignore line endings and indentation. Today, however, practices that made sense in 1957, when computers were the size and price of office towers, may not be all that sensible.

For one thing, if we let our computers notice program layout they would have a better chance of understanding what we mean. That would help them catch our errors sooner. The force of tradition, though, is strong; like ancient scribes economizing on calfskin, today's programmers are still fretting far more over reducing the computer's effort than their own. Perhaps in unconscious revenge they then pass on that pain to consumers of their software.

Putting It All in Context

Today's computers need to be told things that we don't. When we hear that a friend has moved to Edinburgh to help build a bridge, for example, we don't ask whether the friend's legs are also in Edinburgh. We also never think to ask whether there's air in Edinburgh; and we needn't be told that starting to build the bridge by placing a girder in midair isn't a good idea. Today's computers, however, know nothing but what we tell them; legs, air, and gravity are new ideas. They have no preconceptions. This actually isn't such a bad thing if you happened to be a paraplegic building a bridge in orbit, because then legs, gravity, and air would all be irrelevant. Sometimes our prejudices, so useful in day-to-day life, get in the way of clear thinking.

The trouble is that although the computer has no preconceptions, we have many. These preconceptions fit together to form our context—what we know about reality. They're so basic that we can very easily forget them. Whenever we do forget one while using our computer, however, the software blows up.

Without context dependency, it would take us forever to say anything at all. Our normal conversations would become as bad as programming a computer—tedious, time consuming, and frustrating. The meaning of everything we say depends on many things—things in our vicinity, our past, our imagination, sex, race, culture, nation, our humanity. Having to spell out all our references to each other the way computers require would make communication impossible. For instance, we can say "The chicken is ready to eat" and mean either that the chicken (which we have just cooked) is ready for us to eat, or that the chicken (which is our experimental specimen) is ready to eat its food. The meaning changes if we say *potato chip* or *elephant* instead of *chicken*, because of all the things we know about ourselves, eating, time, potato chips, elephants, and chickens.

Because we're always aware of context, we can drop a lot of words that computer programs would much rather we keep. Today's software isn't very aware of context, so it can't handle ambiguity and therefore forces us to add those unnecessary contexts. No wonder it's so hard to use. Everything must be spelled out.

Not allowing for context is bad enough, but the current generation of computer pidgins compound the problem by not letting programmers use redundant expressions when describing contexts. That forces today's computer programs to be so minimalist that, if anything anywhere is wrong, the whole program is wrong. Changing a single letter or punctuation mark in a program could make the whole thing meaningless. Imagine Tolstoy putting the finishing touches on *War and Peace*, misspelling one word, and thereby turning the whole book into gibberish. With no redundancy to use as a cross-check, trying to build a millionline program today is like trying to build a kilometer-high house of cards without glue.

Minimalism is valued in computer languages because it is—supposedly—more efficient (at least for the computer). On the other hand, all other languages we use are very redundant. Even if we lose half of what someone says we can usually deduce what's meant. (Fr xmpl, yu cn prbbly rd ths.) Similarly, today's airliners have three independent backup power systems, and the space shuttle carries five different control computers—in case any one of them fails. That's also why banks make us write out the amount for our checks in both numbers and words. They know we aren't perfect. Apparently, today's computer pidgin designers still don't.

Because most pidgins don't allow redundancy, almost any sequence of computer commands is legal. Consequently, the computer can't distinguish meaningful sequences from meaningless ones. It can only use its rigid language rules to see whether each statement—by itself—is legally possible. To let it catch our errors we would first have to make our programs redundant enough to let it *find* our errors.

The consequences of having no context and no redundancy in present-day programming are that programmers must exhaustively explain every tiny detail and be ultra-precise in doing so—requiring a deadly combination of extreme patience and hyperattention. Thanks to the way we construct computer pidgins, today's computer is an Old Testament god with an awful lot of fussy rules—and absolutely no mercy.

The unwillingness to exploit context and redundancy in computer languages will, however, eventually fade. Programmers today are like chauffeurs were a century ago. At the turn of the twentieth century, a study predicted that there would never be more than two million cars in America, because only two million Americans would ever agree to be chauffeurs. Some people, reasoning the same way today, conclude that programming will never become any easier; it's too technical and demanding, they say. They forget that we made it that way, so we can change it. Of course, fifty years of doing something one way makes any change hard. Even so, the number of machines—and tasks they can perform—are exploding so fast that we're forced to make them easier to use. We must eventually get rid of the chauffeur. It's time for our computer pidgins to grow up into true evolvable languages. They must start learning on the job, because not even programmers can think of everything. What we can say easily limits what we can think easily, which, in turn, limits what we can do, either easily or at all.

The History of the World

The past is but the beginning of a beginning, and all that is and has been is but the twilight of the dawn.
H. G. Wells, *The Discovery of the Future*

History in the computer world divides into seven epochs, moving from the absolute outer darkness of the Second World War and on into the garish klieg lights of the twenty-first century.

Prehistory (before 1945)
Nobody had computers to play with. Nothing happened.

The Paleolithic (1946–1964)
Computers existed, but they were far too unreliable, expensive, and hard to use. In those near-prehistoric times, almost nobody had computer access. Even halfway through the Paleolithic there were no commercial computers at all. All computers were one-of-a-kind laboratory instruments, all finicky prototypes used almost exclusively for warmaking or

scientific research. They were so big and expensive that a priesthood grew up around them to protect and serve them—and to bask in their reflected glory.

The tail end of the Paleolithic, however, saw the first primitive computer languages and the first commercially successful minicomputers.

The Neolithic (1965–1971)

Computers got a bit easier to use with some reasonable, but still primitive, languages. The machines were steadily becoming cheaper but were still much too costly and unreliable for most uses. Most of them were ungainly behemoths needing lots of care and attention. The priests continued to keep everyone else's hands off; making the computer easier to use would only threaten their status.

Toward the end of the Neolithic, some computers were finally given keyboards and screens. Programs that made operating the machine easier were then also becoming common.

The Dark Ages (1972–1981)

The microprocessor was born and languages began to improve a little, although many people still had to use punch cards and other Neolithic technologies. In those ancient days, computers were still largely confined to big corporations, universities, and government installations. Nonetheless, there was a massive movement away from military and scientific tasks and toward commercial and financial ones. The priesthood began to wither, although its dying hand continued to control how easy computers were to use.

Toward the end of this period, prices plummeted and power skyrocketed. Commercial personal computers appeared and punch cards vanished almost entirely.

The Middle Ages (1982–1992)

Personal computers existed, but they didn't have enough memory or speed to do anything really useful, and they were too big and clumsy to carry around comfortably. Software tools were still pretty bad, but at least they were now fairly common.

At the very end of the Middle Ages, portable computers finally became practical. Although they were still pricey and had weak batteries and poor screens, millions of normal people started using them.

The Modern Age (1993–present)

Computers continued to get cheaper and better, faster and smaller, and stronger. They also started talking to each other across international networks. They almost had enough memory and speed to start doing something really useful. They were still unreliable, although less so than before; computers continued to crash regularly, for the stupidest reasons.

Still, improved, less detailed languages were becoming a little more common. Rudimentary handwriting- and speech-recognition systems appeared in portables. Useful computers had almost become cheap enough for most middle-class families in advanced countries to afford one.

They shrank in size to the minimum needed for us to use them comfortably. A notebook became the portable of choice. Big dinosaur computers died like flies in a snowstorm. High-powered computers reached paperback size. Enormously good graphics machines went on sale as children's video games. Now little Timmy or Janie could get for Christmas something that would have supported a multimillion-dollar graphics lab ten years before.

The price of high-caliber computers had steadily dropped from the price of jumbo jets to that of houses, cars, and, then, refrigerators. Today—still plummeting—they are approaching the price of expensive toasters. Massive memory, high speed, and tiny machines are now facts of life. Hardware prices continue to tumble, while power and reliability skyrocket. The price of software, however, has not kept pace with hardware's cheaper prices. It remains hard to use and is still handmade.

The Future

In the future, computers will be much better. They will be a million times smaller, cheaper, and faster, have a million times more memory, and, best of all, be a million times easier to use, because they'll no longer be stupid enough to do exactly as we say. They'll more often do what we actually mean. Software won't be handmade anymore.

In that future, computers will be as common as shoes. Everyone will have at least one, itself made of many, perhaps millions, of smaller computers. They will become lifetime companions; we'll all get one at birth, take it everywhere, and use it for everything. Some will be pets, and we'll probably ask them to fetch sticks and frisbees for us. Cats, of course, will continue to ignore us.

4

The Subjunctive Mood

The art of programming is the art of organizing complexity, of mastering multitude and avoiding its bastard chaos.
Edsger Dijkstra, *Notes on Structured Programming*

A common mistake that people make when trying to design something completely foolproof is to underestimate the ingenuity of complete fools.
Douglas Adams, *Mostly Harmless*

Human territory is defined least of all by physical frontiers.
John Fowles, *The Magus*

Why is programming hard? Getting a computer to do what we want, programming it, means building a very special kind of machine—an immaterial machine. A hotel, similarly, has such a machine. Of course, it has various physical parts too: staff, plumbing, walls, beds, and so forth—that's its hardware. To see to its guests' widely varying demands, though, it also needs a set of procedures for the staff to follow, describing how to handle check-in, towels, room service, and lost luggage. That's its software. The hotel's hardware is useless without the hotel's software, and vice versa. Neither of them alone is a hotel.

A hotel's software, however, is harder for us to perceive than its hardware. Although the procedures control the movement and interaction of physical things, they themselves are intangible; we can't see them, bite them, or fondle them. They're happening in time—not fixed in space—so they're hard to notice (unless something goes wrong). Still, they're just as real and just as important as the plumbing or the lights. Further, those procedures often slip into the background, because the one thing we easily notice about them—the language they're described in—is mostly irrelevant to how they work. Although some languages may make for shorter or more graceful descriptions of particular hotel procedures, the actual language they're described in just isn't important. As long as the staff understands it, it can be Spanish, Japanese, or Urdu.

Finally, whether hotel management chisels these procedures on clay tablets, stores them in computer memory, tattoos them on the staff, or skywrites them every morning, as long as the staff can decode them they're equally effective in running the hotel. In other words, their physical form isn't very important. This makes them easy to change and transport—and copy. Such software could use almost infinitely tiny amounts of energy to store, change, or copy. How it's stored doesn't much matter. How it's expressed doesn't much matter either. The only important thing about it is that it describes processes—sequences of events happening in time.

Computers are still new enough for us to think of programming as an unusual occupation. But it isn't unusual at all, because we're all programmers. Anyone who works out a sequence of actions—whether running a hotel or bringing in the harvest, doing laundry or putting away the groceries, making dinner or handling the nation's money supply—is a programmer. Programming means first figuring out how a process should unfold in time and then creating a how-to manual about the process. The only thing new about it is that these how-to manuals are read by machines. What makes it hard is that the manuals can become immensely complex.

Mean What You Say

A program tells a computer how to do something by giving it a series of instructions, many of which are conditional tests: *If* this is true, *then* that will happen; *otherwise* the other will happen. So programming means building a long chain of what-ifs. It's an exercise in hypothetical thinking, an exercise in using the subjunctive mood.

Most programming today consists of sitting down before a blank computer screen (or a blank sheet of paper), cursing a bit, and thinking about the problem we want solved. Most of the time we're thinking thoughts like: "If we make it do this when this happens, then what should we make it do if that happens?" or "When this condition is true, it should do that, until the following happens." That sort of thing rapidly becomes tiresome and way too complicated. If the problem we're trying to solve is at all interesting, the only way to have a hope of getting it right is to chop it up into pieces small enough to reason about independently.

All programmers do the same thing: We divide the job into pieces if we can, solve the problem on the pieces, then combine what we've learned in solving the pieces to solve the overall problem. But while tricks like that help us make efficient programs when we know what we're doing and can break a problem up into small independent pieces, they don't help us make flawless programs when we don't. To see why, imagine the innards of a wind-up alarm clock. Next, imagine one with a hundred times as many parts, all clicking, winding, whirring, spinning, and ticking together. Then try imagining one with a hundred million times that many parts. That's how complex our most complex computer programs are today.

We can't afford to build a clock with a million parts. For one thing, it would be as big as a house. Yet a few dozen physical parts controlled by software could simulate the effect of millions of different parts. The software tells each part what to do and when to do it. Consequently, replacing hardware by software can make our machines smaller, cheaper, and more capable but not any simpler. If anything, it makes computers more complex, because we need so little energy and raw materials to make them more capable that we simply keep adding functionality. This leads to problems: they can eventually get more complex than we can truly understand.

For example, one common air traffic control computer system in use today contains over six hundred thousand instructions. Of these, almost forty thousand are what-ifs. At each of these points in the program, the program can take one of two or more directions. Just to write the number of different ways to move through such a program would take almost twelve thousand digits—and that's just the number of possible paths. The programmer must also ensure that every single path leads to a correct result. It's like trying to play a pinball game with forty thousand independently controlled paddles. To handle each new pinball correctly, every paddle in the game would have to be reset to exactly the right angle at exactly the right time—and millions of new balls can come in each second. One tiny mistake—anywhere—could cause hundreds to die in a fiery midair collision. Think of that the next time you fly.

We can't build such a system as one giant piece. It's too complicated. Even if we could build it and could test a million possible paths through it every second, checking the whole thing would still take far longer than the earth will last. In software, the word *astronomical* doesn't begin to describe the number of ways to fail. So we don't test all the paths in any big program. We can't. Whether we test it for ten days, ten years, or ten centuries, we can never fully verify that any big program is correct.

For this reason, we build large programs in parts, cross our fingers, and hope that the parts do what we think they will. We abstract the program and group many special cases into a few general ones, then try to reason about the general cases to build our confidence that the program as a whole will work correctly. Doing it this way usually makes the problem manageable. Sometimes we even get it right.

In the Grip of the Soft Machines

It is said that centuries ago, a magician-rabbi built a clay automaton, a golem, in the shape of a man. The golem had great strength and blind obedience but was inert until the rabbi slipped into its mouth a roll of parchment containing a verse from the Torah. As soon as he did so the golem came to life and protected the Jews of Prague from pogroms. Without its software, the golem was only a cleverly contrived statue. Without their software, computers too would be useless hulks, just as hotels would be empty buildings.

That confuses us, because most of us think of something as "a machine" if it hurts when we drop it on our foot. By extension then, "a computer" becomes just a bunch of hardware. We think that because it's easier for us to notice things than to see processes. We see milk, we see butter, but we don't see the churning. We can weigh a car, but we can't weigh a traffic pattern. Yet identifying a computer merely with its physical parts is like calling an office building a hotel just because it has rooms and plumbing. Like a hotel, a computer isn't just a physical thing; it's a cooperating set of pieces of hardware and software.

Ultimately, then, we have trouble understanding computers because we have trouble understanding software. It's hard for us to comprehend software and its power because it's essentially intangible. And, because it's usually removable, it's hard for us to think of it as an integral part of the machine. After all, we can't remove our own brain and survive. Still, software *is* integral. It's the sole reason why computers are far more than just upmarket calculators. Software is at the root of the computer's magic, because computers understand whatever their software lets them understand, which can be anything we understand. Their ability to run any arbitrary piece of software lets them do anything we can imagine clearly enough. That's what makes them so very special.

Adding software to hardware makes a computer into a new machine. That more abstract, but very real machine blankets the bare physical computer, hiding some of its ugliness behind a more pleasant facade and making it easier to use. Software lets us do more with less.

So programmers are a special breed of engineer. Like other engineers, they must first decide what their hypothetical machines need to have, then find ways to realize those needs as extensions of currently available machines, whether hard or soft. Unlike most other engineers—who build mostly physical things like dams, refineries, and dynamos—programmers only need to turn an all-purpose machine into a special-purpose one. In addition, they have the luxury of using words, instead of steel or concrete, to do so. So programming is much more like writing, sculpting, or painting than it is like building a house. No other engineers have machines they can turn into helicopters or toasters on a whim.

When we use a word processor, for example, we're really using a word-processing machine. That sophisticated yet highly specialized machine is built on top of lower-level but more general-purpose machines, which are in turn built on top of even more lower-level and even more general-purpose machines in a huge pyramid of layers; finally, we get all the way down to a truly primitive but truly all-purpose physical machine that actually does all the work.

Anyone who then programs that word processor to behave a certain way is also building a machine, a specialized extension of the bare word-processing machine. Anyone else can, in turn, extend that machine, and so on up the ladder of complexity. Although intangible, every single piece of software in that dizzying chain is as real as if it were made of metal, plastic, and wire.

The physical parts of today's computers usually do only simple things (like adding, subtracting, and so on) because it costs too much to build more complex machines in hardware. If we could afford it, we could just as well build the extensions to the bare machine in hardware, which would make it obvious that they are as real as lawn mowers. Doing so, however, would lead to million-part alarm clocks the size of houses and the price of small European countries. It's far easier and cheaper to build these extensions in software. Thus software is replacement hardware; it lets us trade brain for brawn.

Their ability to turn word into deed is the chief reason computers appear so magical to us. In essence, software is condensed knowledge, and that blurs our normal distinctions between thought and reality. Programming is like turning music into houses.

That brings us one last time to the mystery's heart: Like the golem, a computer isn't just something we can trip over; it's the entire complex of capabilities we've given it, either through hardware or software. It can do anything we can build *or express*. This makes programming a cross between engineering and storytelling.

By the Pricking of My Thumbs

Developing the first computer language translator cost IBM eighteen programmer-years in 1957. Nowadays a small group of university students can do the same thing in a few months. Sounds impressive, doesn't it? Well, let's do some arithmetic. It usually takes three students about four months to build a decent translator from scratch. That's twelve programmer-months, a programmer-year. So, in the forty years from 1957 to 1997, we've increased our software productivity by a factor of about eighteen. But, since today's translators are much better than those of the 1950s, let's say we've improved it a hundred times, just to be safe.

A hundred times better. Wow, sounds like a lot. Imagine if pizza got a hundred times cheaper. But that's nothing. In the same time, computer hardware became millions of times cheaper, and that improved hardware is leading us to try solving problems we would have seen as unapproachable even a decade ago. Now that our hardware has improved so much, we finally have the firepower to solve them, but we still don't have the software skills to use that firepower safely.

Suppose, for example, that we have to build a truly complex software system to defend ourselves against warlike aliens. The software will have to coordinate all the earth's defenses and use them in concert to fend off interplanetary attacks. Let's say the program has to be a thousand million lines long, which is not completely unreasonable; the latest screen-management systems for personal computers are already tens of millions of lines long.

The trouble is, though, that we can dream about a thousand-million-line program, but we can't possibly build one and expect it to work well. Many companies in the software industry expect the average programmer to generate no more than about twenty blemish-free lines of computer instructions a day—around five thousand a year—regardless of the computer language being used. So to build a thousand-million-line program, a lone programmer would need to live about two hundred thousand years. The aliens probably won't wait quite that long before they attack.

Okay, you say, we'll simply do what we do for big hardware projects like dams and bridges and space shuttles: we'll hire more people. But even if we muster a superhuman effort and put thirty-two thousand programmers on it (just about all the American professional programmers alive today), then—going simply by the numbers—they'll still take about six and a quarter years to create the program. Will the aliens wait that long?

Worse yet, even if we could pay that much and wait that long, building software isn't much like building dams. The more people we put on a software project, the longer it takes. And the time needed doesn't rise arithmetically, it rises geometrically, because communication costs go up roughly as the square of the number of people working on a project. Anyone who has chosen a movie at the video store appreciates that two people take more than twice as long as one to decide, and the more of us there are the worse the bickering gets.

That happens because our brains are only so big. We naturally work in groups of no more than about four or five, because we can manage the complexity of that amount of interpersonal communication. Even a group as small as twenty to twenty-five people usually breaks up into at least five groups of at most five; typically one person from each group is chosen to communicate with the other groups. Most of the world's military, for instance, works just that way. Each additional layer adds more communication—and more complexity. Every new employee has to be brought up to speed on the project's state. Then there are the inevitable meetings to decide what must be done and to argue about what was just done. That's why, for example, we have Brooks's Law: *Adding more people to a software project only makes it later.*

Accordingly, some of the biggest software systems to date are being produced by only about two hundred programmers working for five to ten years. And their systems are only around five to ten million lines long. Inevitably, as conditions change over that period, customers' needs change too, out of all recognition. So once a problem gets complicated enough, programmers can't expect to be left in peace to build a program in the traditional way. At current rates of progress they'll never produce flawless thousand-million-line programs. The aliens would crush us before we even got around to deciding on the specs for the proposed defense software.

Building big software systems in tiny steps the way we do it today is like trying to use jewelers and watchmakers to build nuclear power stations and aircraft carriers. It's as doomed as trying to build a space shuttle with handicrafts, bits of raffia, and needlework. We'll only make real progress when we can automate much of what we now call programming.

Longing for the Future

Today we release software and hardware and use customers as testers to uncover their flaws. In essence, we develop successive versions of a system to help us learn what we should have known in the first place. And the bigger the system, the less we understand what we need to do. Imagine if civil engineers built bridges or houses that way. Would you live in such a house? Of course, getting a new computer system to work well isn't like building yet another house, because each new project is just that—new. So the problems are often new.

Programming is about building castles in the air—castles that have to work. They must have plumbing, lights, and a garbage-disposal system. We can't really compare computer programming to house building, however, because house builders don't have to worry about many, many things. They don't have to fear that gravity will be turned off one day a week, or that air pressure will suddenly halve, or that a tornado might suddenly form in the living room. They don't have to design a single house that works well for Bedouins, Tibetans, Eskimos, astronauts, and Jacques Cousteau. They don't have to ask whether the toilets will work in zero gravity, whether the faucets will flow in the Antarctic, or whether there are any termites that eat ferroconcrete.

Physical laws, the terrestrial environment, and normal time scales limit the problems house builders have to worry about. No such limits apply to software. Because we can ask software to do anything we can think of, it can get really complex really quickly.

Further, when builders finish a house, that's it. The buyer doesn't call them up next month and ask them to turn it into an igloo. But that's exactly what happens with software. Giving people a computer system always results in unforeseen complications, and the bigger the system, the greater the complications. Armed with a new computer system, we start doing things we couldn't do before simply because it was too much trouble. Consequently, the demand for new uses booms, leading to demands on the system far beyond what its designers thought it would have to meet. In other words, as the new system lets us see what *could* be done, we react to what it does, well or badly, and demand changes. Very often, solving a problem with a computer simply changes the problem.

City planners have to face the same problems of complexity. For example, the M1 roadway around London was intended to reduce the traffic in and around the city. It did indeed shortcut the routes through London's crazed snarl of streets; so, of course, everyone started using it. Consequently, traffic on the M1 slowed to a crawl, and, soon, Londoners were calling it the world's largest carpark.

So the problem isn't really inherent in software or in hardware, but in complexity itself. Our biggest problems have now grown so complex that we simply don't understand them. When customers first explain what they think they want, computer engineers can't be sure that it's what they really want. After a complex piece of software is introduced, everybody has to work hard to adjust it to handling tasks nobody understood well before it came out. Further, once the software is available, customers' demands on it change. Its own existence changes the problems we ask it to solve.

Today, it's normal for big software projects to cost tens of millions of dollars, be months or years behind schedule, and double or triple their cost estimates—or be cancelled entirely. Even when finished and working successfully, they still have errors. Some computer systems have grown so complex that attempts to patch them up merely result in more flaws showing up elsewhere. That's why it's becoming standard practice simply to leave known flaws in place rather than trying to fix them. Thanks to the complexity barrier, large-scale computer programming has become as hard as politics.

Gaining Power by Losing Control

Today's software isn't easy to make or change, to fix or understand, to use or reuse. It's as if every violin were a Stradivarius, and you could only play one you built yourself. You'd have to have built it recently, too, because otherwise you wouldn't remember how to work it. Even your own old Strad would be useless. Yet nothing inherent in computers makes them this rigid. They are what we've made them, and we can change our minds. They would become better tools if we gave them more autonomy, making them able to adapt for themselves.

Today we have total control over our computers. They're like mechanical horses that can't take a step unless we say so first. But total control is good only if we can foresee all the possible problems and never blunder. Unfortunately, fifty years of trying to build complex computer systems has finally forced us to realize that we're slow-witted, tiny-brained bunglers. We simply can't track all the myriad details involved in solving a very complex problem.

Nor is that reality a new concern; politicians too know it well. Over twenty-five hundred years ago, for instance, when writing of state governance in his *Book of Ethics,* Lao Tzu, the reputed founder of Taoism, said:

Intelligent control appears as uncontrol or freedom. And for that reason it is genuinely intelligent control. Unintelligent control appears as external domination. And for that reason it is really unintelligent control.

Taoist governors don't have to tell farmers when to feed their ducks, nor village ratcatchers how to catch rats. Taoism assumes that change is fundamental to life. Rigid, fixed rules make no sense because conditions are always fluid. No set of fixed rules, no matter how elaborate or how well thought out, can guide us through all the situations we might meet. Taoism gives us the freedom to respond to life in whatever way is necessary at the time without always having to make precalculated responses to events.

Our current programming practices work best when our problems are small enough and well defined enough for us to fit them into our heads in their entirety. They fail when our problems grow bigger and more complicated than that. To hope to solve more challenging problems, we'll probably have to give up some of the control over our computers that we now hold so dear. We must let our horses help us find the correct path. We must become Taoist programmers.

That kind of talk scares many people. They're afraid that if we make computers more flexible (assuming that we can do it), we won't know for sure what they're going to do next. Well, they're right. What they don't seem to realize, though, is that our biggest computer systems are now so complex that we already can't predict exactly what they'll do next. It's unlikely that the space shuttle launch-control program—all quarter of a million lines of it—is flawless. Nobody's perfect.

What I Tell You Three Times Is True

We often fail to solve a new problem the first time we face it. Consider, for example, how we're busily paving over most of the earth's arable land at a time when our population is exploding. Once upon a time, all our present-day cities were tiny villages located near rivers, deltas, valleys, or arable coasts. They had to be, otherwise they couldn't exist at a time before food could be airlifted anywhere. Having once settled there, we stayed in the same places and brought up our kids; then they brought up kids, and so forth—which is why all the best land is now being covered by concrete. Pioneers always blunder; it's inevitable.

We design most programs today so that they too are always pioneering. To them, it's as if every time we use them is the first time. They can't remember the past, so they're condemned to repeat it. Consequently, today's computer users—who, of course, do remember the past—are forced to ignore it. Programs that keep no history of their past can't change their behavior over time. It doesn't matter how many times we go through the same sequence of actions, such programs never see that we want to do the usual thing. They can't. With no memory of the past, they can have no idea what the usual thing is.

Now, think about the muscles in your right arm. The more you use them, the stronger they get. With its structure fashioned over millions of years, a muscle works as if it assumes that, as you've used it a lot in the past, you're likely to use it again in the future. Conversely, the first time you use a muscle after not using it for a while it's very weak. Now why do living things work that way? Why, for instance, aren't all our muscles always at their peak of strength? Wouldn't that be great? Well, such perfection is good only when you know you've already arrived at the perfect body design. That perfection, though, is a kind of death, because it leaves no room for change.

Living things aren't always at their peak of performance. They know they have an energy budget and that they can't predict everything. They can't afford to prepare for every possibility, so they compromise. They develop their technology in such a way that if it becomes necessary to change, there's some way for them to do so. For example, most of us catch colds every year, but we rarely suffer from the same cold twice. Our immune system can't predict which cold viruses are going to attack each year, so it does the next best thing. It waits for the assault then deploys nonspecific cold-fighting technology that tries to outgeneral the current virus. Once we catch a cold, we retain that specialized defense against it, and the next time it strikes we just shrug it off.

So living things are adaptive; they learn as they go. Our present-day computer systems aren't like that. Buy a computer system today and five years from now it'll be just as stupid as it is now. We don't let it flounder and gradually get better the way we do. We force it to always do the same thing in the same circumstances. That would be fine if we were as infallible as our computers. But we aren't. We blunder all the time. Furthermore, our errors are usually characteristic—if we do something one way once, we're likely to do it that way again. It would make sense to let our computers pay attention to our past mistakes, because that might help them understand our future mistakes better. After all, we're sure to keep making them.

Many computer programs have already run hundreds of millions of times. While doing so, they've seen lots of human error in all sorts of variations. Why don't they save any of that information? If they did, the next time they ran they would know a little bit more about us and so could change their behavior to adjust to us. If they paid attention to the mistakes we usually make, they might be able to save us effort in the future.

That can't happen today, because in our quest for total control we don't let computer programs change their behavior over time. Nor can they notice when we make the same sorts of errors over and over again; so they can't help us reduce the consequences of those errors. They *could* remember the past, but we don't let them. Consequently, instead of trying to make our computers adapt to us, we force ourselves to adapt to them. We force ourselves to become machines to use our machines; we—programmers and users alike—have become slaves of the machine. And that's just silly.

There's no point blaming computer pioneers for our present troubles. They chose an inhuman way of using the computer fifty years ago based on constraints they had to live with then, just as earlier pioneers had to settle on arable land. If they hadn't, we wouldn't be here to make fun of them. But things are different today. Thanks to enormous strides in computer hardware, the computer's time is now far, far cheaper than our own. It's no longer cost-effective to force ourselves to be inhuman to use them. Pioneers blunder. Settlers don't have to.

Monkeys at the Keyboard

Up to the early 1980s, most computers were like supertankers. Large and expensive, they served an extremely specific purpose and only highly trained operators could use them. In those days, computer designers didn't much care about computer users, because the very idea of users as distinct from designers was unthinkable. That's all changed now. Today, computing power is cheap and widespread, and users far outnumber designers and builders. Yet perceptions within the computer industry haven't yet changed with the times. Computer people still force computers to behave much as they did in the 1950s. Consequently, the computer's users, you and me, have to jump through all sorts of unnecessary hoops.

Imagine, for example, that you're using a computer program that's patiently waiting for you to give it a word. Suppose the word you have in mind is *Stradivarius*, but you actually give it a slight misspelling, say, *Stadivarius*. Most people would know exactly what you meant but, typically, the program wouldn't have a clue.

As far as it's concerned, *Stadivarius* is as close to *Stradivarius* as it is to *strawberry* or *couch* or *waffle iron* or anything else that isn't exactly *Stradivarius*. Today's computer programmers apparently assume that we're monkeys using a computer. They seem to think that everything we say—unless it's exactly what they want us to say—is equally random. However, if the program had a rough idea of the nearness and farness of words, it could save you time and trouble. If you say *Stadivarius* because you're in a hurry—or because you're dyslexic, or because you don't remember exactly how to spell the word, or because you just spilled orange juice on your computer—the program might be able to figure out what you probably meant.

Not only would that lower your blood pressure—you wouldn't have to be so insanely careful—it would also give the programmer a chance to let the program notice errors you make regularly by seeing how close they come to what you actually intended. Perhaps it could even start noticing patterns in the kinds of errors you make, noticing, for example, when you're most likely to make these errors. Maybe it's just before lunch that your attention begins to flag; perhaps just after lunch when you feel drowsy or when you're using an especially tricky part of the program.

Say you're issuing a complex command and you make an error in specifying one part of the command. Most of today's computer programs would simply beep, forcing you to issue a corrected command. It might happen that as you reissue the command you're justifiably a little annoyed at having to be bothered; so you don't make the original error but do introduce a new error in another part of the command. The program again beeps, issuing some fairly meaningless error message. Once again you issue the command. This time you do the human thing and focus only on the part that caused you trouble last time, completely forgetting the rest of the command. As far as you're concerned, you've clarified your meaning completely. After all, you're used to talking to people, who, based on context, usually understand exactly what you mean. Now, however, because this third version of the command is incomplete, the program beeps for the third time, and your blood pressure soars.

Why couldn't the computer see that if you mess up a command the very next thing you're likely to do is to repeat the command? Further, why doesn't it know that if you mess up one part of a command, the next time you'll probably focus only on that part? If it held onto at least that much context, it would know enough to compare the first two command versions you issued and perhaps be able to extract the correct form of the command you intended. Most computer programs aren't that forgiving— partly because their designers can't be bothered to make them so, and partly because they think it would be too hard to do it. Sometimes it would be, but often it wouldn't.

We all blunder while using our computers—programmers included. When the computer beeps at us, all we can do is curse, because to us it's obvious what we want done—given the context of our previous work. Why can't the computer figure it out too? If you ask most programmers that question they tell you that the computer isn't very smart. It's a mere machine, they say with a superior chuckle; you simply have to grin and bear it. They're just hoping you'll go away. What they've forgotten—or hope you don't know—is that all the smarts the computer has they've given it.

Now, certain kinds of errors we make really do require a very smart helper to interpret them correctly—that's why executive secretaries get paid so much. Many other mistakes, though, aren't that hard to figure out. The computer's programmer could let the computer recover a lot of what we mean by constructing the program to notice our goals and recognize that we're not just fooling around. We have particular problems to solve and always establish contexts for solving them. We aren't monkeys at the keyboard and computers are no longer supertankers.

When Logic Isn't Enough

If we rip out the pages of Shakespeare's complete works (about a quarter of a million lines of print) and glue them together end to end, they would stretch for about a kilometer. Today, even the software for a small telephone exchange would be around two kilometers long; the space shuttle's onboard controller's about four kilometers; the *Hubble* space telescope's about eight kilometers; and a major telephone exchange's over sixteen kilometers long. And Shakespeare didn't have to worry about being consistent, correct, or complete.

During the birth of modern programming forty years ago, building even a simple twenty-page computer program was an enormous achievement; decades later, the birthmarks still show. Once upon a time, a twenty-page program would stress our pathetic little machines to their limits and we had to be extra careful of the machine's time. Nowadays, we're trying to build programs of a quarter million pages with the same software tools, and it just isn't working. We have the hardware to run such large programs but not the software skills to get them right. Thanks to tradition, we're still using the same old clumsy 1960s tools.

This isn't really very surprising. At only fifty years old, computing is still terribly young. Young programmers in the field can still gather round the grizzled old timers—those in their thirties, or sometimes even forties or fifties—and listen to tales of when the world was young. The stories the old timers hand down across the generations tell of a beginning that was a free-for-all; there was no such thing as disciplined programming. Then came some spectacular computer failures—rocketships blew up, chemical plants failed, airplanes crashed. Programmers reached for tools to help tame the ravening beast of complexity and came up with logic.

Their response was entirely natural. Logic was already familiar to the mathematicians, engineers, and scientists building and using the most ancient computers. Besides, many early computer people were themselves mathematicians or physicists, or had strong mathematical leanings. Early on, logic seemed fundamental to computer operations. Best of all, it lent respectability to a young field unsure of itself.

Unfortunately, traditional logic doesn't deal well with things involving inconsistency, redundancy, and changing purposes, which you're always going to run into when working with people. Logic is effective for consistent, precise, and special-purpose thinking because it's deductive and exploitative, not inductive and exploratory. It needs a lot of training and a formal cast of mind, and few of us possess that kind of discipline. The universe is messy and so are we. Developing big computer systems, therefore, is much more like a branch of psychology, sociology, or anthropology than of logic.

What a computer can do is limited by its structure and its programming. Today our imagination limits both. So far, it's been easier for us to build machines that slowly answer precise questions about precise information. More often, though, we want fast, rough answers to fuzzy questions about vast quantities of vague and inconsistent information. Such problems are insoluble using traditional methods. As a result, today's programmers, still thinking too much like logicians, refuse to let software adapt to us. When creating it, they must foresee every possibility and get the right things done in the right order at the right time. They pretend that they can think of everything in advance and flawlessly execute contingency plans for every possibility. And they expect themselves to get it right the first time. Of course, being human, they usually don't. They botch either the plan or its execution. When that happens, the software fails.

In sum, traditional programming works well only when five things are true: First, we know exactly what we want to do. Second, we can foresee every possible eventuality. Third, we can predict a correct action for each such eventuality. Fourth, we can execute each such contingent action flawlessly. And fifth, the solutions we need are especially efficient. As soon as our problems grow big and complex, all five conditions cease to exist. That's our problem today—and it has but one solution.

Shoot the Programmers

I really hate this damn machine,
I wish that they would sell it.
It never does quite what I want,
But only what I tell it.
Anonymous

Because of the way programmers are brought up, they assume that their programs must always do the same thing in the same situation. By definition, such devices can't adapt to user peculiarities. What we really want, though, is something that does something different even if the situation appears to be the same, because—to us—the situation is almost never the same. We see everything in a context that can change from instant to instant.

Programmers can't tell what your current context is when they're building their programs. They can't tell if you're busy today, or restless, or bored. They don't know how much experience you've had with their program or with computers in general. Their training tells them, however, that their programs must behave exactly the same way from run to run. So their only recourse is to try to think up all the different ways that you might want to use their programs, then try to deal with all those possibilities—an impossible task.

Most of today's programmers are like lawyers who are concerned only with law, not justice. Their letter-of-the-law, obey-or-you-will-be-punished tradition has the same problems in computing as it does in law. It's extremely brittle and requires extensive training to follow. The vast majority of us who have a job to do and who lack extensive training in using the machine are therefore continually frustrated. We would prefer using a computer to be more like fashioning a recipe and less like establishing a legal contract. If we're learning Spanish for a trip to Mexico, for example, we don't have to first decide exactly which parts of our brain will do what and exactly how and when they will do it. We simply learn Spanish. With computers we're nowhere near that effortless stage. We must still lead them step by excruciating step to make them understand how to do the simplest thing. Before using them, we must ourselves thoroughly understand the task we want them to do. Then we must explain it in meticulous detail. And we can't ever make even the tiniest mistake, either in creating programs or in using them.

Computer programming has improved a lot over the past fifty years, yes; but the improvement is largely because of major hardware changes. Whereas hardware keeps leapfrogging ahead every eighteen months, software is still lost in the dark ages of the 1960s. Programming is still far too hard. Why don't our computers notice the context of a current piece of work and act appropriately? Why do they make it so easy for us to flounder? Why don't they adapt to us as we use them? In brief, after fifty years of development, why are our computers still so stupid?

Computer hardware is already powerful enough for us to do interesting things, and it's rapidly getting ever more powerful. Besides, most computer hardware today isn't working all the time anyway; most computers are asleep most of the time, snoring away while they wait for us to give them something to do. Thus the current limits on what computers can do lie more in us than in our hardware. What we lack today isn't more hardware, but more imagination.

The change to adaptive computer systems will come, as often these things do, by the actions of a few forward-looking software companies with the courage to take a risk and produce a new kind of software—adaptive software. Only when one of them succeeds will the stampede begin. Then the rush will be massive, because the profits will be outrageous. Tomorrow's profits have always belonged to those who take today's risks.

Inevitably, we'll develop better ways to work with our computers. The whole thrust of computer development has been toward ever-easier use. Now, though, we've about reached the limits of what we can do using our current assumptions about how computers must work. To find new solutions, we'll have to give up something—something important. It may well be the absolute control we think we have today.

To summarize, today's software isn't bad because computers are stupid—although of course they are—but because today's programmers are lost in the past. They still value the computer's time more highly than the consumer's time (and that includes their own programming time). Here's our software problem in one sentence: Programmers don't die as fast as machines do. Hardware can improve as dramatically as it does because every two years we can replace an entire generation of computers with faster, better, cheaper descendants. We can't yet do that with software. It's still being handmade.

The obvious way to make it better is to follow Shakespeare's advice in *Henry VI* and shoot all the programmers, then start over from scratch. Since we're unlikely to do that anytime soon, our software will remain hard to make until we learn how to make it more adaptive. When we do, though, it will start improving even faster than our hardware has. Then things will really start popping.

5

Limits to Growth

Life is the art of drawing sufficient conclusions from insufficient premises.
Samuel Butler, *Notebooks*

One cannot live forever by ignoring the price of coffins.
Ernest Bramah, *Kai Lung Unrolls His Mat*

There is no problem so large it cannot be run away from.
Daniel Keys Moran, *The Long Run*

What can't computers do? To find out, we first have to consider some people who think abstractly for a living—mathematicians. The problems they fell into and the way they got out of them have limited our own ideas about the possibilities of computers ever since.

For about three thousand years—until almost the end of the nineteenth century—mathematicians were at play madly inventing the future of their discipline. Always thinking of their subject as the path to absolute truth but rarely trying to prove that it was, they weren't ready for a kick right in their complacency. By about 1900, though, they were in deep trouble. And they knew it.

The problem they finally had to face head on was the problem of paradox, one that had been around in mathematics for a long time. About twenty-four hundred years ago, Zeno, a Greek curmudgeon living in Italy, gave the early mathematical world four paradoxes that bedeviled mathematicians for the next two millenia. One of his paradoxes proved, essentially, that you could never leave home because to cover the distance to the door you would first have to cover half the distance to the door. To do so, you would first have to cross half that distance (a quarter way to the door), and to cover *that* distance, you'd have to walk half that distance, and so on. Because there would be an infinite number of points to cover between you and the door you would never reach the door.

Here's a slightly more sophisticated example of a paradox: Suppose you have an apple tree that bears an infinite number of apples. One day at eight minutes to noon you pick two apples off the tree, label them 1 and 2, drop them on the ground, then pick up and eat apple 1. At four minutes to noon you pick two more apples, label them 3 and 4, drop them on the ground, then pick up and eat apple 2. You keep doing that an infinite number of times until noon, halving the time interval at each step. At each step you pick two new apples and eat one old one. The first step takes four minutes, the second takes two minutes, the third one minute, the fourth thirty seconds, and so on. You complete an infinite number of steps before noon. How many apples are on the ground at noon?

Well, you might argue, since you picked twice as many as you ate, there must be an infinite number of apples still littering the ground. On the other hand, for any particular number, you ate the apple labeled with that number sometime before noon; so there are no apples on the ground. On the third hand, as you could never really carry out the task, perhaps the answer is *undefined*. Or perhaps *who cares?*—after eating all those apples you're much too sick to care. Which is it?

Hmm, that's odd. Here's a seemingly simple question that appears to have no answer. It appears to be a paradox.

Paradoxes abound in time-travel stories. Say you invent a time machine; could you use it to go back in time and kill your great-grandfather? If you could do that, then you wouldn't have existed to later invent the time machine to do that. Or, again, say you build a time machine from some strange blueprints you find, then go back in time to hide the blueprints that your later self will find. If you could do that, then who made the blueprints in the first place? It's all very confusing.

Turn-of-the-century mathematicians found mathematical paradoxes just as confusing as we do, and they knew they didn't need a time machine to create one. By the late 1890s, many paradoxes were showing up in the most fundamental parts of mathematics and mathematicians were dividing into almost religious opposing camps. Even apparently simple questions not involving time or infinity can lead straight into the rank bowels of paradox.

For instance, if a town only has one plumber and that plumber fixes the pipes of all the townspeople who don't fix their own pipes, then who fixes the plumber's pipes? Let's say Fiona is the plumber. If she fixes her own pipes, then she, the plumber, can't fix her pipes. But if she doesn't fix her own pipes then she *is* a person who doesn't fix her own pipes; so, as the plumber, she must fix her own pipes. She must both fix and not fix her own pipes. All she can do is be really confused.

Paradoxes sound mildly amusing when phrased in terms of plumbers, infinite apple trees, and time machines, but they aren't so amusing when phrased in terms of logic, because that logic is sometimes our only way of telling whether nuclear missiles, say, will work. The heart of the problem of paradox is that something doesn't necessarily exist just because we can talk about it in well-formed sentences. Good grammar doesn't guarantee good sense.

While paradoxes might merely make good party puzzles for most of us, mathematicians absolutely loath them. If you've been working on something for twenty years and suddenly a paradox turns up in your logic, then your entire world turns to quicksand. In the world of mathematics, if your method of reasoning fails anywhere, it fails everywhere. To a mathematician, a paradox is like used chewing gum—just as sticky and twice as unappetizing. Paradoxes caused so much fear and loathing for mathematicians that by 1900 a German named David Hilbert, the greatest mathematician of his age, had had enough. He wanted a completely infallible, purely mechanical method anyone could follow to show that although some deeply flawed piece of reasoning looks reasonable, it is in fact nonsense. Armed with such a method, he thought, he could banish paradoxes forever. He sought a foolproof way to turn disguised nonsense into patent nonsense. He failed utterly.

Leap Before You Look

To keep mathematics safe from paradox, Hilbert built on the most foundational parts of deductive mathematics laid down over two millennia before by Thales and Pythagoras. He tried to turn mathematics into a meaningless deduction game. In Hilbert's method, we're first supposed to build an abstract machine to solve a problem by choosing some assumptions and rules. Then, like turning the crank of a sausage maker, we just keep grinding through all the possible deductions resulting from combining these rules and assumptions in various ways until we solve the problem. To keep ourselves from unconsciously assuming something false (and so falling into the unforgivable sin of paradox), our cranking must be completely mindless. We're not supposed to use our intuition, change our minds halfway through, or add anything to our procedure. In other words, we were supposed to act exactly as today's computers do.

For example, we could turn arithmetic into such a sausage maker by postulating the existence of the numbers zero and one and by giving rules to define how to add, subtract, multiply, and divide. As we mindlessly turn the crank, these two assumptions and four rules would then produce $2 + 2 = 4$, and $12/3 = (5 - 4 + 1) \times 2$, and every other arithmetical result whatsoever—no matter how complex—all without relating anything to the real world of four sheep and twelve cows, and so on.

The only meaning of any of the mathematical tokens used in that game—whether 2 and + in arithmetic, *line* and *circle* in geometry, or *derivative* and *integral* in calculus—derive from the way they're used in the game's rules, nothing more. Hilbert's idea was to make everything follow only from a few fixed rules and assumptions, which is exactly the way today's computers work.

For computers following a program, and supposedly for mathematicians playing Hilbert's deduction game, the game's tokens have no content in themselves. They aren't *about* anything. In such a world, the plus sign, +, for instance, has nothing whatsoever to do with adding one apple to one apple and getting two apples. It's merely two crossed bars whose meaning is defined only in terms of other tokens in the game. Of course, after a mathematician proves something using such tokens, physicists or engineers or other crazy people may choose to ascribe meaning to it in the real world, but that's their lookout, not the mathematician's.

Epitomizing that idea, the English mathematician and philosopher Bertrand Russell wrote:

If our hypothesis is about *anything* and not about some one or more particular things, then our deductions constitute mathematics. Thus mathematics may be defined as the subject in which we never know what we are talking about, nor whether what we are saying is true.

That was the wasteland that Hilbert, and most of the rest of the mathematical world, was prepared to turn mathematics into to preserve it from hordes of bloodthirsty paradoxes. They were prepared to give up meaning entirely.

It didn't help.

Jam Today

At a mathematicians' meeting in Paris, on Wednesday, August 8, 1900, Hilbert asked the mathematical world to find fixed, circumscribed, mechanical procedures to solve every mathematical problem and so banish paradox forever. Only so, he argued, could we be sure that a proof was unequivocally correct. As the French mathematician and philosopher René Descartes had said centuries before:

It were far better never to think of investigating truth at all, than to do so without a method . . . by a method I mean certain and simple rules, such that, if a man observe them accurately, he shall never assume what is false is true.

Hilbert wanted a completely mechanical way to solve any mathematical problem; something like directions in a cookbook, only more precise: name these parts, construct those equations, simmer for half an hour, solve for x, y, and z. As a test case of that idea, he asked mathematicians the world over to show that simple arithmetic can never lead to paradox.

What a harmless-looking request. Surely that should be easy enough to prove? The arithmetic of buying and selling, of paychecks and taxes, of chartered accountants and loan sharks is surely consistent. Isn't it? Nonetheless, Hilbert's deceptively simple problem remained unsolved for thirty long years until he retired in 1930. That same year, a Moravian graduate student in Vienna named Kurt Gödel dropped a bomb on the whole idea of avoiding paradox. He showed that if arithmetic isn't paradoxical, then there must be true statements we can't prove within it. Conversely, he showed that if we can prove every true statement within arithmetic, then there are false statements we can also prove to be true. The universe is much stranger than we usually give it credit for.

So even in the superexact world of mathematics, the only field where we can ever hope to know something for sure, either something is true but unprovable, or something else is provable but untrue. In other words, the universe gives us a choice: We can either have a small, correct, but terribly incomplete book of knowledge, or we can have a huge, complete, but wildly inconsistent book of knowledge. We can have completeness, or we can have consistency, but we can't have both.

Which is just as surprising as the uncertainty principle in quantum theory enunciated by the German physicist Werner Heisenberg in 1927, just three years before Gödel presented his theorem. Heisenberg showed that we can find the exact position of a subatomic particle, or we can find its exact velocity, but we can't do both together. "Now we know," Heisenberg said later, "that we shall never know." If we know where we are, then we can't know where we're going; and, if we know where we're going, then we can't know where we are. As Lewis Carroll said about another matter, "Jam to-morrow and jam yesterday—but never jam to-day."

An Exercise in Self-Control

Hilbert's most important problem was to find a precise meaning for a "completely mechanical method," because in his scheme that was what everyone was supposed to use to prove everything else. Essentially, he wanted to know what we can expect any machine to be able to do. The entire mathematical world thought about that problem for thirty-five long years. Then one day Alan Turing—that young and most unconventional English mathematician mentioned in chapter 1—solved it. One lazy afternoon in the spring of 1935, after a long run along the river Cam in Cambridge, the twenty-three-year-old Turing lay down in a meadow and began to dream of machines, a decade before there were any modern computers. By reasoning in a most unorthodox, but quite ordinary way, he had a most spectacular idea.

Consider solving a problem by creating and deleting tokens fixed on some medium, thought Turing, say by writing and erasing letters and numbers with pencil and paper. Obviously, some things don't matter. It doesn't (or shouldn't) matter what color the paper is; whether we write left to right, right to left, or up and down; or whether we're making marks with a pencil, pen, brush, lipstick, typewriter, or toothpaste. It doesn't even matter if we're using paper. We can sense tokens in other ways (say, by hearing them spoken, or by feeling them as in Braille); and we can alter them or add to them without writing (say, by speaking them, or by acting them as in mime or charades). What matters is that we're somehow perceiving tokens fixed on some medium, and we can create or delete them, perhaps based on whatever tokens are currently there, plus some thinking.

As long as the medium doesn't matter, Turing reasoned, let's choose paper and pencil. And, as the actual tokens we choose don't matter, either, let's choose letters and numbers. To avoid worrying about details like margins and line spacing, let's also turn our paper into a ribbon divided into squares and, further, make the ribbon of unlimited length to ensure us of more than enough paper. Now, for simplicity, let's make our tokens so that only one can fit within each square of our ribbon of paper. That way we need only move one square at a time and look at one square at a time. We decide what to do next based on what we're currently seeing and on our current brain state.

But how do we model "brain states"? Again, Turing felt that some things don't matter. It doesn't (or shouldn't) matter whether it's a nice day, whether we're happy or sad, or whether we're in Fiji, in Guatemala, or on the first Mars mission. All that matters is what we're going to do to the tokens on the ribbon once we get to each brain state.

Now, finally, we can describe the whole computation as a series of small-scale, very specific instructions like:

If you're in brain state 55 and you're currently seeing an *a*, then replace the *a* by a *b*, go to brain state 226, and move left one square.

That format looks terribly restrictive, but it isn't really. First, instead of changing state we could have stayed in the same state. Second, which state we go to doesn't have to depend on what we're currently seeing. Third, instead of writing a *b* we could have left the *a* alone, or we could have written any other token from our pre-fixed set. Finally, we could have simply stayed put. These are all the choices we have at any one step.

What makes Turing's scheme interesting is that we can have as many steps, states, and tokens as we wish (as long as it isn't an infinite number). So the computation can get very complex—complex enough, for example, to control a jumbo jet, or a nuclear power station, or an aircraft carrier. That's exactly what computers do today, just by following hundreds of millions of these small-scale instructions hundreds of millions of times a second.

Turing had managed to capture the essence of all the processes Hilbert and company were willing to accept as "completely mechanical methods." With that single step, he had invented the computer. As soon as he defined his machine, however, he saw some of its limitations. Some problems can't be solved by any computer, no matter how fast it is. In 1936 he proved that no machine, however made, could tell whether it could solve a very special kind of problem without actually trying to do so—and possibly taking forever. That's like saying that we can't tell ahead of time whether we can sail from one place to another, no matter what we know about geography, ships, wind, sailing, weather, or the sea. The only way to tell whether we could sail from Britain to America, for instance, would be to try to do so and possibly get lost forever, without realizing that we're lost.

So, although a computer is a universal machine and can solve infinitely many problems, there are still more problems it can never solve. All computers have limits. But then, so do we.

A Critique of Pure Reason?

The mechanical procedures Hilbert had in mind and Turing gave shape to were definite and fixed. They were well-defined computational recipes that even a mindless robot could follow to make wonderful food. Consisting of fixed sequences of exact and simple instructions for carrying out well-specified tasks, they either solved the problem in a limited time or mindlessly kept doing the same old thing forever. There was no chance of trying something new.

The instructions could be completely described in a limited number of well-understood words and were entirely predictable and unchanging: when faced with the same situation they always prescribed exactly the same steps in exactly the same sequence. They weren't subject to chance, whim, feeling, or intuition. As cooks they would never add salt to taste, because they didn't allow for taste. These procedures were narrowly focused on the problem at hand. They never changed their minds, got lost, hungry, bored, hung over, or distracted. They really had no minds to change. Everything had to be completely planned out in advance so that all eventualities could be handled—minutely, consistently, mechanically.

Unvarying with experience, they were the perfect epitome of what we think of as a machine and, many would say, the perfect antithesis to our own brain. But do computers have to be designed that way? Could we make them flexible enough to slither out of the Hilbertian straitjacket? Computers are made things; we made them, we can remake them.

Lights On, But Nobody Home

Today's computers don't learn for themselves. They usually don't have legs, hands, or eyes; and they don't yet have enough processing power and memory to make sense of what they would see and touch even if they did. Thanks to the history of computing, we build and program them in a way that makes it hard to get them to adapt to us. There's no reason, though, why we couldn't build future machines entirely differently.

Suppose, for example, we wanted to build a robot factory to make robots. Here's how we would probably do it today. We would spend years carefully planning the factory and then rigidly laying it out to achieve high value per dollar spent. The factory would almost surely use some variation of the conveyor-belt system, with many highly specialized, very delicate and demanding, and very expensive robots stationed at different places along the belt. Everything would have to happen at a specified time measured in thousandths of a second. Spatially, each part of the robots being constructed, and the robots doing the constructing, would fit together precisely—perhaps down to the thousandth of a meter. There would be no tolerance for even relatively minor mismatches.

The factory would be very efficient at what it does. But if anything at all went wrong, if anything was even slightly misaligned or mistimed, the whole factory could grind to a halt. Such a factory couldn't adapt to the unexpected and would be useful for nothing but its rigidly narrow speciality. Today, we create computer programs that are just like that.

Now contrast that scenario with the way nature might build such a factory. In effect, each one of our cells is such a factory. If the robot factory were like a cell, its main purpose would be to build and maintain all the robots it contains, not some unspecified set of robots. The factory would exist for the sole purpose of continuing to exist. Anything we wished the factory to do for us would have to be a by-product of its drive to exist—like the honey and milk we trick bees and cows into producing for us as a by-product of their life cycles. This factory would not emphasize efficiency until and unless it had to compete with another factory for resources. Then the efficiencies would only concern particular scarce resources. Any still-abundant supplies would still be used profligately.

Control of the factory would be decentralized. No robot would take an overall guiding role, pressing the buttons to make everything work together. Each robot would be in it for itself. No single robot would have any smarts to speak of. There would be, instead, a great many different kinds of robots, each playing a tiny role. The set of robots would be built in such a way that any given part or connection in any one robot would be handled by many other robots. If the part was never attached for one reason or another, too bad; the resulting robot simply wouldn't function the way it was supposed to, if it functioned at all.

Each robot would be built piecemeal, and the interactions between all the robots would be haphazard. Each robot would be continually roaming about at random, and chance meetings would determine whether two or more robots interacted to help build or maintain another robot. Newly built robots wouldn't necessarily be perfect. If robots exchanged messages, they wouldn't do so by a fixed, direct route or by sending them to a fixed, direct address. Each message, like the robot it's intended for, would wander at random around the factory. If it happened to meet the right robot (identifiable by its shape), it would attach itself and in some way alter what the robot did. In essence, a message would itself be a robot.

There would also be scavenger robots roaming about trying to dismantle other robots. Not only would these scavengers attack inactive robots, they would also chew on any active robots they happened to meet and become attached to. Waste-disposal robots would rid the factory of any unsalvageable parts cluttering up the place. Everything would be continually on the move, continually being built or dismantled.

No single copy of any robot, therefore, would exist for very long; instead there would usually be many copies of each robot. The actual number of copies of a robot around at any time would be proportional to its current importance to the functioning of the entire system. No single robot copy would ever be so important that it couldn't be dispensed with. Several robots would also exist only in blueprint form. They would be built only when needed and, once unneeded, would be unceremoniously scavenged for parts. The design of each kind of robot would have arisen through small successive random changes to the stored blueprints for that robot; and the blueprint mutation would be ongoing, so that new kinds of robots would be continually produced.

To defend against floods, earthquakes, and fires, the factory would need damage-control and repair robots. It would have ingestion robots to extract useful work from some energy source. For long-term survival, it would require storage robots to reserve some of the extracted energy for later use in emergencies. It would also have foraging robots to find and process raw materials. Foraging robots from other factories might attack the factory to steal its resources and make more copies of themselves; or they might take the resource back to their own factory—which comes to the same thing. So the factory would have to have defense robots, and perhaps attack robots.

If the factory's own foragers came upon another factory, the two factories might develop a mutually beneficial trading arrangement. If the trade became so important that it developed into a symbiosis, each factory's welfare would become the direct concern of the other. Eventually, such interacting factories might even band together in bigger and bigger groups, implicitly identifying themselves as one superfactory by a complex and interlocking series of symbiotic arrangements. The superfactory would then have a single common purpose—joint survival—and would become, essentially, a living thing.

To a traditional engineer, the whole system sounds wacky and inefficient. Yet it's the system that made and continues to maintain us and all other living things. It's how we're built and how we work. Although it's extremely inefficient, its great advantage over the highly specialized and totally efficient artificial system described earlier is that it can adapt to many changes in its environment. We could one day build—or perhaps a better verb is *grow*—computer programs just like that.

Lessons from Reality

The more specialized anything is—whether it's a snail, a tobacco plant, a Panda bear, a factory, or a political ideology—the less adaptable it is in the face of change. Few of our engineered products, and almost no natural systems, are that brittle. Take one brick out of a bridge's foundation and the bridge still stands; but take a brick out of an arch and the whole arch falls. Take away one leg of a table and it still stands (usually). Take away one leg of a tripod and it falls. We build most of our computer systems more like arches and tripods than like bridges and tables.

Think of a pond versus a swimming pool. A swimming pool has clean, sharp lines, clear, continually chlorinated water, artificial aeration and circulation, and regular visits from pool cleaners. A pond has none of those things. On the other hand, a swimming pool takes an awful lot of energy to maintain, while a pond is maintenance free. And, although pond scum may look disgusting, unpolluted pond water is about as drinkable as swimming pool water. Perhaps more so, for we evolved in an environment with ponds, not chlorinated swimming pools.

We build computer systems today to be perfectly adapted to the problem at hand. Because we key all their responses to all the situations we can foresee, when they meet something we didn't foresee, they fail utterly. Today's computer programmers, in effect, live in a world of three-legged chairs and pristine swimming pools.

Of course, nature has enormous resources—much more than we have. It has a whole planet to play with, and millions of years in which to experiment. Our computer hardware will probably never be as extensive as nature's is now. So we can't simply ape nature's workings and hope to develop more flexible computer systems anytime soon. Still, we might be able to use schemes similar to the ones that arise biologically—if we design them cleverly enough.

To a biological system—whether a cell, a bacterium, a plant, a fungus, an animal, an immune system, an ecology, or the entire evolutionary system—nothing is graven in stone; everything is up for renegotiation. In nature, there are no failures—only feedback. "Errors" are only opportunities for learning something new. Furthermore, chance events mediate every biological process, from building a molecule to developing an ecology, from regulating a heart valve to the process of evolution itself. Thanks to decentralized control, internal competition, contextual dependency, high redundancy, imprecision, and a direct connection to the real world, biological systems are the world's best adapters. They adapt to whatever happens that's new—unless it's an extreme change—and life continues. If our computers are to get much better and help us solve really complex problems, we'll probably have to make them adaptive too.

An End to Innocence

Two balloonists are lost in the clouds high above the Andes. Afraid that they'll drift out to sea, they frantically release some of the balloon's hot air to descend and find out where they are. As they descend they make out a man smoking a pipe on a hilltop.

"Where are we?" they shout down to him. The man with the pipe pauses reflectively then says, "You're in a balloon." He then ambles away.

"That must've been a mathematician," says one balloonist to the other. "How do you know?" asks the other. "Three reasons, really. He thought carefully about his answer. What he said was absolutely true. And it was of no earthly use to us."

It's always easier to look for solutions using tools we understand, even if it means looking in the wrong place, because looking in the right place could mean having no tools at all. So our first steps in any new field are always the same: we bring to bear all we know from other fields to try to make sense of the new stuff. Eventually though, we run up against several barriers as we discover—surprise, surprise— that the new field isn't exactly the same as any of the old ones. Only then do we need to invent new tools to work in it. That's our problem today.

To find a new path for modern computing we're going to have to re-examine Hilbert's fundamental assumptions. To save mathematics from error, he wanted a foolproof way to solve all problems, a method that would never go wrong and that anyone—no matter how ignorant or stupid—could follow. Although he never knew it, he was asking for computer programs. Out of Hilbert's seemingly crazed request, through Turing's genius, came the machines we know today as computers—the most obtuse, most uninformed information manipulators around. Before making Hilbert's ideas live, however, Turing had to kill two important things about the way mathematics, or any other human pursuit, is carried out.

First, he had to severely restrict the class of problems his machines could be asked to solve. To use his machine to solve a problem we must first be able to express the problem completely and precisely. If a problem isn't expressible in a limited number of precisely fixed and well-understood words, no part of it can be solved with his machines. Turing didn't design his machines (at least, not initially) to solve open-ended problems that might take forever to fully specify. For example, they weren't designed to solve the riddle of life or control a living thing throughout a lifetime of experience; the problems of meaning and survival change too much from day to day.

Second, Turing had to pretend that when we first try to solve a problem, we already know how to solve it. Of course, we often don't know any such thing. Often we aren't even sure what the problem is, exactly. We certainly don't first deduce the whole solution in all its complex detail, then follow a prescribed course. If authors had to do that before writing their books, for example, we would have no books.

Consequently, when we first try to solve a new problem we use intuition, feeling, and hunch—in other words, our experience. An intuition comes from remembering lots of little pieces of information that seem somehow related to the current problem. The relation isn't obvious, though, or easy to state; we may not even be consciously aware of it. Nor is an intuition always true. Yet it's true often enough to give it some value. Like a detective putting the pieces together, we come to a solution by, consciously or unconsciously, seeing lots of little things that add up to one big thing.

So we, faced with complex, ill-formed, ever-changing problems, try many different things before hitting on a way to solve a new problem—if we ever do. Whether we are aware of it or not, we reason by analogy to other problems we've seen. Once Turing's machines get going, however, we don't let them revise their procedure in the light of new evidence or insight. We never let anything new occur to them, and we deny them access to the history of earlier attempts.

Luckily, what's wrong with computers isn't in them; it's in the way we use them. There's no reason we can't use Turing's machines to solve more complex, open-ended problems. First, though, we have to change how we think about computer programming.

Writing in Water

A woman goes to a psychiatrist complaining that she's been married three times but is still a virgin. The psychiatrist asks her why.

"Well," she says, "My first husband turned out to be gay and wasn't interested, the second was too old and died on our wedding night, and the third was a programmer."

"Oh?" says the psychiatrist, "What's wrong with him?"

"Well," she says, "Everything was fine except that he never stopped explaining how good it was *going to be.*"

Today's computer professionals think of programming as making a system perfect beforehand, rather than perfecting the system in place. Consequently, our computer programs are quite inflexible. Yet if we could let them be more grounded in the real world, more open-ended, more independent, and more fallible—in other words, more like living systems—they might eventually become quite competent at handling new problems. To do so, however, we'll probably have to make them small and fast and let them make mistakes from time to time, just as we do.

A computer program that deliberately makes mistakes is anathema to the present generation of computer engineers. Even so, fallible, yet small and fast computer programs could help us find the truth by pooling many pieces of partial evidence—we might even call them intuitions. Each piece of evidence, each hunch, is useful, even if it doesn't settle the question at hand all by itself. If we're willing to give up some of our fixed ideas about how computer programs must work we might gain flexibility in many ways.

First, we could get better information from an intuition-style computer program by simply running it over and over. Of course, that would be senseless if the program always did the same thing. If it were to vary what it does, though—even in the same situation—and if its average behavior were successful, we could reduce as much as we wish the chance that it might blunder.

Consider, for example, the way this works in the judicial system. Our courts have on occasion jailed the innocent and freed the guilty. Ideally, the justice system should never err, but that's impossible in practice, because knowledge is always incomplete. So, to reduce the risk of being wrong, we have appeals courts. Each successive trial is meant to be an independent test of the defendant's innocence. Of course, each trial isn't really independent—unless we can find aliens to serve on the jury. If each trial were independent, however, after many of them we would grow fairly confident about the defendant's guilt or innocence. Out of our inherently flawed process, we have fashioned a tolerably certain one.

Second, intuition-style programs could give us some idea of the truth much faster than the more normal, massive programs that try to account for everything all at once. A partial answer that arrives on time is worth more than one that is accurate out to fifty decimal places but arrives a month late. Fast and crude is often better than slow and accurate. Turing's machines, of course, usually have the luxury of as much time as they want (as long as it isn't infinite time) before they have to respond. Not so for us. All living things have deadlines. We always have to make do. When playing tennis we can't stop the ball in flight and spend hours calculating the exact racquet position and force we need to return a fast serve.

Third, if we had many intuition-style programs, all different, we could run all of them at the same time and let the answer with the most votes win. With these kinds of programs, the more computers we could throw at a problem, the faster we might get an answer. For instance: You're walking in Bengal, India. You spot a swiftly moving yellowish blur. You smell something rank. You hear a sort of coughing growl. *You start running*—because you're about to be attacked by a Bengali tiger. Probably. No one of the things that your senses report to you, or that your knowledge of Bengal tells you, conclusively proves that. But putting them all together makes you almost sure. Besides, if you're wrong, you'll just have gotten some exercise. If you're right, you could avoid being lunch. We make all our decisions the same way, whether in ten seconds or ten years, because we never have complete information.

Fourth, if each intuition-style program were independent of the others, then many programmers could create several of them independently; this would eliminate the communications among programmers that slow down the programming process. So with these kinds of programs, the more programmers we could throw at a problem, the faster we might get an answer. For instance, while searching for a number with a certain property, one mathematician might report that the number is less than ten million. Using different methods, another might calculate that it must be divisible by fifteen. Using still other methods, a third person might find that it's greater than nine million. Taken separately, each mathematician's method restricts the number only a little. Taken together, their three pieces of information limit the possibilities greatly.

Fifth, intuition-style programs could be easier and faster for programmers to create. Because each little piece—each intuition—only nibbles at the overall truth, the complexity of each program would be much lower than that of a giant program that tries to swallow the truth whole. For instance, we get our news from many sources. We listen to the radio, watch television, read the newspaper, talk to friends, and so on. No single one of those news-gathering schemes tries to give us all the news there is. We don't spend the entire day in conversation, nor do we watch television all the time (well, most of us don't, anyway). If television broadcasters had to cover all the news there was, they would have no time to do anything else. Besides, they couldn't do it—the task is far too complex.

Sixth, incrementally building solutions by adding more and more intuition-style programs would let our solutions be much richer and more responsive to change. If we gained a new and major insight into a problem, we would only need to add a new intuition-style program in a way that tells the whole suite of programs to treat its guesses more seriously than those of the others in the suite. We wouldn't need to restart the whole problem-solving process from scratch, the way we must when we build large new programs all of a piece. A suite of intuition-style programs would, therefore, be easier for programmers to adapt to changing problems by giving them more choices.

For example, when we want to move things, we can do it by car, truck, rail, plane, ship, or skateboard. To talk about eating we can use any number of words that once meant almost the same thing: *dine, eat, feed, fare, devour, ingest,* and so on. Different but overlapping things, whether they're transportation systems or words, are redundant and seem wasteful; but they compete with each other for business and so become more efficient at specialized things. Further, each one takes up some slack if a competitor fails; consequently, the system as a whole almost never fails entirely.

Seventh, programmers could allow a suite of intuition-style programs to develop a graduated response by letting some parts of the suite prepare the way for other parts. One small piece could be a scout for other pieces that might use far more time and effort than it does. Scouts could act as quick filters to determine which of the more complex (and slower) parts should try their hand next. Similarly, television executives wishing to produce a new show don't spend all their money making the entire series at the start. That would be too much of a risk. Instead, they take a little money, produce a pilot episode, and air that. If the public responds well, then they spend a little more money on a few episodes. If the public likes them, only then do they commit a lot more money to a run of shows; and so on. By the same token, we don't usually marry the first person we meet but meet many people briefly, progressively diverting more and more time to those we found most agreeable on the last pass.

Nor are military forces likely to attack all at once; they go in in stages, committing more and more resources to areas where the enemy is seen to be weakest.

Eighth, programmers could let a suite of intuition-style programs adapt itself—at least part of the time. The decisions of the suite would then be influenced by the partial answers given by the component programs that have most often guessed right in the past. Over time, it would learn to attend more closely to those parts that have most often guessed right in the past. We do something like this when we expect more from successful people. A bestselling author has a better chance of getting a new book published than an unknown author. A television show we know to be amusing is more likely to get our attention than one we found boring the last time we watched it. A successful movie spawns imitations, variations, and sequels. (Of course, that isn't necessarily a formula for high creativity.)

Finally, programmers could let a suite of intuition-style programs copy successful parts of itself, changing them slightly to get even better performance. Or it could copy parts of two or more independent pieces and recombine them to form new pieces by a kind of machine sex. We would then have the bare beginnings of a self-evolving programming system.

The Rag and Bone Shop of the Heart

You can only find truth with logic if you have already found truth without it.
G. K. Chesterton, *The Man Who Was Orthodox*

Despite the many attractions of a more biological style of computing, it will take a great effort to change the way we do things. We design today's computer software to better exploit yesterday's computer hardware, and we design tomorrow's hardware to better serve today's software. So each cycle locks us tighter and tighter into the python's coils. We're slowly strangling on the consequences of our own past decisions.

In the beginning, when vacuum tubes roamed the earth, the computer was so expensive, and its time and memory were so precious, that computer folk became biased toward extreme formality and predictability.

With so much money chasing so little computer technology, that enormous selection pressure kept up. Now, decades later, computer people are still determined to predict and control every last thing about any process they're trying to automate.

It's hard not to be that fanatical when you're faced with a machine that never messes up and never lets you avoid the consequences of your own messes. When dealing with each other we're used to an awful lot of latitude, because we're good at understanding what others want no matter how much they garble what they say. With the computer, however, our every error boomerangs straight back to us, then lies at our feet staring up with accusing eyes. As a result, people only become computer programmers if they're obsessive about details, crave power over machines, and can bear to be told day after day exactly how stupid they are. Naturally, they take more personal responsibility for events around them than others do. They know that if anything goes wrong—anywhere—it's entirely their own fault.

There's a special fierce joy in programming computers today that nonprogrammers simply can't comprehend. Programming is one of the few nonmilitary, nonmedical vocations on earth in which you absolutely, positively must know exactly what you're doing at all times. Like a bomb-disposal squad, a programmer works under the actinic glare of an infallible and merciless taskmaster who refuses to let even the slightest mistake slip by. So, while others can pretend to understand something by writing a book or telling a story or giving a speech, only programmers are required to know exactly what they're doing, in all its enormous and intricate detail, all the time. Some of the best computer programs we have today are simply elegant poems told in logic. That's Hilbert's real legacy.

Looking back over the trail we've covered so far, we can see that the limits of computers lie mostly in the limits of our own imaginations. Computing is the way it is today because of its history in mathematics and philosophy, the history of its hardware's technical limitations, and the economics and sociology of making, selling, and protecting software and hardware. Early success at solving important practical problems—like how to shoot down enemy aircraft before they bomb you flat or how to mass produce and sell machines made of slow and clunky hardware—froze the approach into the one we have today. But that doesn't make it the only one possible.

Hilbert tried to reduce all of mathematics to meaningless deduction. Turing then tried to reduce all of problem solving to meaningless token manipulation. Both acts of creativity were terribly important for getting us to this point; but neither fully captures the complexity and richness of the original subject. Today's computer engineers are the direct inheritors of Hilbert's worldview. His view of mathematics, however, is about deductions *from* a theory, while science, like life, is more usually about inductions *to* a theory. Scientists build theories to try to explain and predict the things they see happening around them. In life, though, there's never any guarantee that those theories are correct.

Solving a problem or creating a program isn't a one-time thing like stamping out yet another cookie with a cookie-cutter. It's more like making a horseshoe. First we bang on the molten metal, then let it cool into a fixed shape; if it's not right we reheat it and bang on it some more. It's an act of creation. Similarly, the most important parts of programming are far messier, and far more interesting, than some trivial and mechanical checking of all the possibilities. Rather than ineluctably progressing from brute ignorance to the nirvana of total knowledge, programming, like all other human pursuits, backs and fills. All human knowledge grows only by conjecture and counterexample, criticism and correction, guessing and failing.

There's no absolute certainty in mathematics, just as Heisenberg and his cronies showed that there's no absolute certainty in physics: "Now we know that we shall never know." Outside of blind faith, there's no certainty anywhere. The best we can hope for is piecemeal attempts at the truth, always provisional, always uncertain. Apparently, though, somebody forgot to tell that to computer engineers.

Paradox, inconsistency, and doubt are all inevitable if you're going to try to understand the universe with only limited time, knowledge, and other resources. Like physicists, or philosophers, or anyone else, mathematicians don't have—and never will have—certainty. Always groping in the dark with the rest of us, they can only be guided by their intuitions of the inherent beauty and rightness of things. Yet the work progresses anyway, despite the fog of uncertainty through which we all stumble. Lacking certainty, mathematicians simply shrug their shoulders and get on with it. Like life itself, mathematics is a fallible and supremely human process of always becoming, never of simply being. That's what computer programming will eventually become, too. We'll eventually have to give up our Hilbertian total-control philosophy and let our machines be more adaptive. Because we're already losing control.

6

Thinking About Thinking

They sought it with thimbles, they sought it with care;
They pursued it with forks and hope;
They threatened its life with a railway-share;
They charmed it with smiles and soap.

Lewis Carroll, *The Hunting of the Snark*

To attain the impossible we must attempt the absurd.

Miguel de Unamuno

There is always one moment in childhood when the door opens and lets the future in.

Graham Greene, *The Power and the Glory*

Could computers think? Today's computers definitely don't think in any real sense. They can follow any well-defined series of simple steps, no matter how long it is, but no one knows how to design a sequence of steps that represents what we would call thinking. That doesn't mean it can't ever be done, though.

On a bright July afternoon in 1874, Reverend Charles Lutwidge Dodgson, better known to the world as Lewis Carroll, was in Guildford ministering to his cousin and godson, who was dying of tuberculosis. On a ramble in the Surrey countryside that afternoon, Carroll thought of the line "For the Snark *was* a Boojum, you see." From that one line he eventually built a long nonsense poem called *The Hunting of the Snark: An Agony, in Eight Fits.*

His poem tells of a motley crew of strangely ridiculous people who go in search of a snark, a mythical creature none of them has ever seen. They're not exactly sure what snarks are good for, only that they can be eaten with greens and are handy for striking a light. Having no real idea of how to find a snark, they try various absurd methods of catching it. Many amusing misadventures later, one of them, unfortunately, accidentally meets a snark. For that snark was a boojum, you see.

The questers didn't know exactly what they were searching for, and they tried lots of wacky ways to find it. Eventually they found it, by accident. And when they did, they wished they hadn't.

Over the decades, many critics have commented on Carroll's poem, some seeing its influence in James Joyce's *Finnegans Wake* and others in T. S. Eliot's *The Waste Land*. A good deal of literary ink has been spilled arguing over it. Today, though, it may be better to think about the poem in terms of artificial intelligence—our search for a machine intellect that we would consider as smart as ourselves. The analogy is so very apt.

Fit the First

Most of us think of chess as a game requiring great intelligence. Yet, although today's best chess programs play good chess, trouncing all but the very best players, they really aren't all that smart.

Suppose you were such a chess machine. You would have a list of rules describing how the pieces move—the knight goes like this, the bishop goes like that—and a description of the board. Every time your opponent moves, you would look at all the pieces you still have and try out in your head all the possible ways you could legally move. For each possible move you could make, you would then look at all possible countermoves your opponent could make. Each move and countermove would give you a new board position. To get some idea of whether you're better off in each position you would use a lot of fixed tests, like "Am I in check?" or "Am I holding the center squares?" or "Have I lost any pieces?" If you were forced to end the game on the next move, you would choose the move that your list of little tests says is the best.

However, a game usually doesn't end after one move. Your adversary might have a countermove to the move your rules told you was the best one to choose, a countermove that might, after a series of further moves, eventually put you in a terrible predicament. So, before each move you cautiously look into the future for as many more moves and countermoves as you have time for. Then you choose the move that appears to lead to the best position several moves in the future. (You judge which future position is best according to your list of fixed tests.) You make that move. Then, when your opponent moves, you start the whole process all over again.

Today's chess machines look at a monstrous number of possible future chess positions, trying to decide the best current move. But they can't look at all possible positions—there are far too many. Still, they search a lot of positions—over ten million a second for the world's best machines. Human players can't search that much. In fact, they usually don't consciously search much at all.

Perhaps you're now thinking that if chess machines can search so very many moves ahead, they're unbeatable. Well, you'll probably be right in a decade or two; but for now the world's twenty best human players still often trounce the world's best chess machines. There are many reasons for this; here are two of them. First, not even grandmaster chess players know exactly how they decide which positions are good. So the fixed tests chess machines use often give only a rough estimate of each position's goodness. Second, even chess machines can look only so far ahead, which is why they sometimes fall into traps laid for them by grandmasters. Weak human players often blunder in the same way.

However, one or two decades or so from now, some chess machine, somewhere, will probably become the world champion. Soon after that, playing chess against a machine will be like boxing with a bulldozer— it's possible, but what's the point? Still, that won't mean that human intelligence will be usurped. All that will happen is that tournament rules will change and human chess players will come to competitions armed with machine assistants.

As no human player can analyze very many positions into the future, all players bring other weapons, other parts of their personalities to the game. Some are aggressive, some are timid, some are gamblers, some are pedestrian. All play in their own unique style; by doing so, the best of them don't simply play chess, they create art on the chessboard. Today, chess machines don't usually do that. They play with no heart. Playing by fixed rules defined before the game begins, computers rarely adapt them as opportunities arise. They never get angry and forget something, or get greedy and fall into a trap, or get terrified and collapse under a relentless assault. And they never, ever show compassion or pity or remorse for a clearly beaten foe. So don't look to these machines for any trace of emotion. At least, not anytime soon.

In sum, we would consider a chess machine smart if it didn't just solve the problem of winning at chess but did so in a clever way. We would be even more impressed if it came up with its strategy all by itself. It wouldn't hurt if it could get to the tournament by itself too. Today's chess machines, of course, do none of those things. Consequently, although chess is still considered a problem in artificial intelligence, few of us see today's chess machines as smart.

All this illustrates a general rule: As soon as we understand a problem well enough to program a computer to solve it efficiently, we cease to think of it as part of the field of artificial intelligence. Artificial intelligence, in effect, is in the business of putting itself out of business.

More and More About Less and Less

It surprises many of us that computers with the right programming can fix machines, search for oil, identify chemical compounds, and do all sorts of other specialized things. In various restricted domains, some computer programs can outdo highly trained petroleum engineers, research chemists, and doctors. For example, special medical programs can diagnose many diseases. To see how they might work, suppose that a group of you are deep in the Amazon rainforest and one of you gets sick. If no one has medical training, what do you do?

First you notice that your companion has a certain set of symptoms, and you look them up in that big medical reference book you happen to have with you. Someone had compiled the book by looking at the symptoms of lots of patients with lots of diseases. Suppose it says that if the patient has spots and a bad attitude then it's either measles or deep depression. It also says that there's an infallible test to tell the difference: all past measles sufferers have turned blue when whacked on the knee, whereas all patients with deep depression just got mad.

So you whack your friend on the knee and, depending on the outcome, you've diagnosed the disease. Now that you know the disease you can treat it (presumably by using that other big book on rainforest plants you've thoughtfully brought along). That same trick of compiling a list of all previous causes and symptoms can work in prospecting for oil, fixing a car, or selling stocks and bonds. You, plus a suitably compendious book, equals an expert on each of these subjects.

Of course, you can foresee the problems. Who updates the book to add new diseases? Who writes it in the first place? What if your patient's symptoms don't exactly match any of those described in the book? What if you don't notice all the patient's symptoms? What if the book is wrong? What if the suggested treatment isn't available? What if many of you are sick? Whom do you treat first? What if it's an emergency and you must decide all these questions in a hurry? None of today's software systems can handle all these questions. As you can see, there are many problems with today's simplistic artificial intelligences. If you have to choose between a competent human expert and a machine, there's really no choice at all.

On the other hand, not all human experts are competent. Further, human experts can't be around all the time. Those of us who can't pay a good doctor to live in our homes would far prefer even a mediocre medical software system we can call on day or night to nothing at all. Good doctors are few, and they sometimes need sleep. Furthermore, good human experts are expensive. Although the first commercial artificial intelligence systems were quite rudimentary, and usually cost several million dollars, they saved some companies millions of dollars a year, every year. Their development costs plummeted even more once we knew how to improve them. Their costs keep falling, while salaries just keep rising.

A computer program is certainly more obedient than a human employee. It can't be suborned or hired away—you can't bribe software. It never gets tired or sick, hungry, or hung over (although its expertise can get old). Copying and distributing software costs pennies and take seconds, whereas producing a new human expert takes decades and costs hundreds of thousands of dollars. In addition, a program's capacity can rise quickly—although it can't yet reach the level of competence a human expert can eventually attain. A program is very useful, but it has its limits.

The Pretense of the Real

Nobody knows what intelligence is. So how could we tell if our machines have it? According to legend, Odysseus had a similar problem. As a boy, Achilles had been hidden among some women for fear that if he were found he would die, as prophesied, in the Trojan War. As the war started to heat up, Odysseus came looking for him. But Achilles' face was so fair, and his disguise so good, that Odysseus couldn't tell him apart from the women he hid among. Clever Odysseus then disguised himself as a merchant and offered for sale some women's ornaments and a few weapons. As only Achilles handled the weapons, Odysseus knew who he was and took him off to Troy, where, after much to-ing and fro-ing, great deeds, and whatnot, Achilles was, inevitably, killed. So it goes.

The point is that Odysseus, having no easy way to tell Achilles from the women, invented a test that, in those days anyway, no young man could fake. Today, we're more or less in the same position as Odysseus was way back then. We really don't know what we do when we're thinking, so the only reasonable thing seems to be to test anything claiming to be intelligent, just as we unconsciously test each other. If it can fool us for long enough, it seems reasonable to assume that it's intelligent.

Let's see how that might work with proving personhood. Imagine that you're having a nice, warm, intimate conversation with your twin sister. You're holding hands and she's sitting so close to you that you can see the pores in her skin, hear her slow breathing, smell her perfume, and feel the warmth of her body. The two of you are talking about shared interests, close friends, family, and childhood sweethearts. You have absolutely no doubt that you're talking to another person.

Now imagine that you're talking with a stranger far away in space, time, language, and culture. Suppose, for instance, that you're talking to a distant stranger on a ham radio. Because you don't know how to use a ham radio, you have to talk through a translator to a radio operator who only speaks French. The radio operator is sending out the message in Morse code. At the other end, your correspondent, who speaks only Urdu, has to talk through a translator to a radio operator who only speaks Russian. What with all the various transcriptions and translations, there's a delay of several days between statement and response. Are you still sure you're talking to another person? Almost all the cues you normally use to determine personhood are gone. You can't smell, touch, see, or even hear your correspondent. You can't listen to a voice or read some handwriting, you can't see a shadow or feel a breath on your cheek. Now, you ask yourself—What sex is my correspondent? What age? What race? Could my correspondent be a made thing—a machine?

That scenario isn't so farfetched, either. Millions of us using today's computers have the same problem every day, except that we usually don't think of it. When receiving electronic messages from someone we don't know and can't see or hear or smell, all we can do is read the words. If we think about it at all, we might test our correspondents by asking questions and observing responses. Lacking a good definition of intelligence, that's all we can do.

With Forks and Hope

Of all doctors, psychiatrists have the toughest job of any in the medical profession. Every problem that no one else can diagnose as a specific ailment of the leg or heart or nose gets shunted to a psychiatrist. Only when science advances enough to identify an organic cause for some ailment previously thought of as psychiatric does it cease to be solely a psychiatric problem and enter the realm of some other specialty. For example, we've only recently learned that bacterial infection—not stress—causes most ulcers, and that brain structure—not anxiety—causes most stuttering.

Similarly, artificial intelligence researchers, who get all the problems other computer people can't yet solve, are just as confused as psychiatrists. Faced with a mishmash of problems, tools, backgrounds, and philosophies, the artificial intelligentsia is splintered. The trouble is that just because something is hard for us it isn't necessarily hard for computers, and vice versa. We invented them to do something we're bad at; they can do arithmetic with unparalleled speed, reliability, and accuracy. So it's only fair that they're bad at things we're good at. The surprise is that they're bad at such apparently easy things.

Arithmetic, high-speed or otherwise, isn't something we're born knowing. Nor is it something most of us learn easily. On the other hand, recognizing faces, telling men from women, speaking, understanding speech, recognizing and grasping objects, and walking around without bumping into things—all are easy for us but hard for today's computers. Unfortunately, most of us aren't very good at math; so we think that solving equations, say, is hard, while recognizing faces is easy. We unconsciously assume, therefore, that computers must be very smart. Actually though, it's the other way around—solving equations is dead easy and recognizing faces is terribly hard.

This is not at all surprising, considering human evolution. For example, a three-month-old baby can do an enormous number of things even our most sophisticated computers can't yet do. That's only surprising if we imagine that an infant is newly made. In actuality, a three-month old baby isn't three months old; it's three-and-a-half-thousand-million years and three months old. That's roughly how long the baby's ancestors have been adapting themselves to cope with the universe and each other. That experience, the result of millions of years of unconscious and opportunistic trial-and-error learning by millions of creatures, is incorporated into the child's being.

Mathematics, science, and all the other things we try to teach this ancient infant as it grows up are very recent inventions. They're much easier for us to teach to our computers because within our recent history (the last five thousand years or so) we started to think about them abstractly. In other words, algebra is much easier for us to program than speech because it's about half a million years younger. Consequently, the only school that teaches us anything truly important is nursery school. We almost never have to teach a child how to breathe, eat, cry, sleep, walk, talk, recognize Mom, socialize, and most importantly, learn. About all we do is try to pass on how to do these things in socially acceptable ways.

These abilities were essential to the child's forebears, and some of them—eating, for instance—go all the way back to the first life-forms. So evolution had a hand in coding the structure that makes it easy for that child to learn how to do these things. That huge span of evolutionary experiment, though, has not dealt with such recent inventions as the alphabet, arithmetic, calculus, and all the other more abstract pursuits we pride ourselves on today.

Recognizing faces is something we're very good at, almost at birth. We're so good at it, in fact, that we even see faces where there aren't any—in clouds, on the moon, and on Mars, now that we can take a really good look at it. We recognize faces quickly and easily because we come prepackaged with advanced face-recognition hardware developed and fine-tuned over millions of years. Accordingly, nearly two-thirds of the nerve cells in the part of our brain just behind our temples respond to faces to some degree.

It was essential to our survival long before we evolved into humans to recognize one face out of many—or any face out of a background—so that we could recognize our mother's face and quickly tell friend from foe. We needed high-speed face-recognition hardware to recognize and evaluate the emotional state of others in our troop. It was essential to staying alive when young, and finding a mate when mature, to recognize immediately the current attitude of mothers and other caregivers, receptive mates, and dominant males. We get some of that information from scent, posture, and gesture—and, for the last quarter of a million years or so, from language. Most of it, however, comes to us through faces. Smiling or snarling, growling or moaning, the face is the window to the mind. Thus face recognition was subject to strong selective pressure long before we became human. Through that enormous pressure, our facial muscles became ever more complex, diverse, and expressive, so that we could broadcast our state of mind more clearly. Today, our faces have the most highly articulated and controllable muscles of any part of our bodies.

By contrast, for most of our evolutionary development we had no need to solve equations. So the kind of abstract thinking needed for arithmetic, algebra, and logic are hard for most of us. Instead, we're evolved to survive in a complex and rapidly changing world. Our ancestors had to guess quickly what a vague shape or sound meant so as to take evasive action. Those who didn't, died. We're survival machines, not logic machines. That's the essential problem for artificial intelligence. We can watch birds to see how they fly, and we can model fish to see how they swim; but what works well for flying, fighting, farming, and so on fails for thinking. Because we have no idea what we do when we think, we can't simply create a computer program that does the same thing.

The only way for such a program to develop seems to be the way we developed it ourselves—through a long period of trial and error in a rich and constantly changing environment.

Basic Instincts

Most of what we know about our brain comes from centuries of watching the effects of drug overdoses, strokes, brain tumors, age, genetic flaws, and head injuries. In the last generation or so we have developed technology that lets us experiment on live brains; but even now, by using microelectrodes, we can only listen to the traffic going through a few nerve cells at a time. More recently, using brain scanners, we've been able to watch the whole brain at work, but only from the outside and on a gross scale. Our tools are still very primitive, compared to the brain's immense complexity. For example, we lose thousands of brain cells a day, never to be replaced. That doesn't much matter, though, for our brain is very redundant—perhaps precisely because it must deal with that loss. A slowly growing brain tumor can destroy 80 percent of the nerve cells responsible for hand control before the hand becomes paralyzed.

Trying to understand the workings of the brain is like trying to predict the flow of cars, water, electricity, and sewage in a city the size of a planet. Today's clumsy tools are the equivalent of putting a couple of dozen microphones at a few major intersections and listening to traffic noises; or taking satellite snapshots of the planetary city; or waiting around for natural disasters, like gas explosions or floods, and then looking at the effects on traffic flow a few months later. With such primitive tools, we can immediately see a few broad patterns—like rush hour and the difference between day and night traffic. We can also see a few patterns within the patterns—like the difference between weekday and weekend traffic. But that's about it. We certainly can't predict exactly where a particular car might start from or end up, or what exactly a burst water main, say, might do to the overall traffic flow.

We've learned a lot about the brain, but there's so very much we still don't know. Why, for instance, do most of us look up when we're trying to remember something? Is it cultural—something we learn as we grow up? Or is it physiological—something basic to our structure? Kissing and handshaking are both culturally learned, for not all cultures share them. Hugging, pointing, grooming, and marking territory, on the other hand, aren't. We share them with many other primates. We also know why we put our hands on our hips when irritated—it's to make us look bigger and more threatening. But when we talk on a voice-only telephone and gesture, to whom are we gesturing? We know that using extracts of crushed plant genitalia as perfume is a cultural practice, because not all cultures do it; but why do we blink more when we're nervous? Why do we scratch our heads when we don't know something?

There are so many mysteries. We don't understand genius, we don't understand why we dream, we don't know how we store memories, we don't know how we can will our muscles to move, or how we experience pain or hunger or nausea subjectively. In fact, we don't know how we manage to fashion a subjective experience at all. We're adrift in an ocean of mystery.

Talking to Yourself

Where are you? Are you in your brain stem, which is helping you keep awake and breathing right now? Or are you in your thalamus, since it's helping you decide what to pay attention to? Perhaps you are in those language areas of your brain that are helping you make sense of these words. Or are you in your forebrain, the region that helps you speculate, plan, and worry? Or in your hippocampus, where you store and recall memories? Or even in the memories themselves, since they are what makes you you? Without any of these parts you wouldn't be you. So where are you?

There appears to be no single place in the brain where you are you. After more than a century of study, no brain-damaged victim has ever had localized damage resulting in a loss of decision-making ability. Such losses do happen, but they always result from damage to many different areas of the brain. That's not really very surprising, for it's likely that our brain was built by an unconscious, random process that had no way to retrace its steps and try out radically new designs. It's so complex and highly redundant because every part of it evolved to exploit some particular historical accident or physical limitation over the course of millions of years. The bits and pieces that work together to produce what we call intelligence probably evolved separately and for different reasons. Slowly, over eons, they joined together.

Intelligence, then, is most likely a very large set of highly specialized skills rather than a unified thing unique to each individual. We can therefore imagine the brain as more like a pomegranate than an apple—a series of centers with no central core or controller telling the parts what to do. Like a swarm of bees, the brain has no place you can point to and say, "Look, here I am," just as you can't point to any one bee in a swarm and say that's where the swarm is.

Which brings us to the question of what is the mind. In normal speech we often use the word *mind* in a mystical way. Many take it to be the seat of consciousness; a sort of supernatural, immaterial entity that actually is us—something that's apart from, yet lives in, our brain. In scientific circles, however, that use of the word *mind* is now archaic. Freeway traffic jams might help explain why. Sometimes when we're driving on a freeway, traffic around us slows down, and we must slow too. After a few minutes, we speed up again, because all the cars around us are magically speeding up. Often we can't find any reason why there was a slowdown in that area. Why?

A freeway under moderate traffic is like a hose full of water, and an accident is like briefly pinching shut the hose. Stopping the flow results in a blob of slow-moving water molecules backing up just behind the pinch. Now consider what happens when we release the pinch. Fast-moving water molecules just behind the slow-moving blob will slow down because the water in the hose is slightly denser near the blob. Molecules just ahead of the slow-moving blob, though, will speed up, because there's no longer an obstacle to free movement. So the blob's front is decaying while its rear is expanding. Consequently, a blob of slow-moving molecules moves backward down the hose, against the flow of the water and away from the pinched spot, even though it's always made of forward-moving molecules. The blob is a like a memory of the pinch, persisting even after the pinch is gone and slowly degrading over time as more and more fast-moving molecules bustle through it. The blob isn't any particular set of water molecules; it's a pattern of temporarily slowed molecules. Like bees in a swarm, it's something that arises from the molecules' interactions but isn't itself a molecule.

In a similar way, the mind, as opposed to the brain, isn't so much a *thing*; it's more of a *way*. The sequence of brain events happening in time, the dance of the individual bees within the swarm—change, and growth, and decay—make up the mind, not its physical components. We don't need a supernatural agency to explain the mind's intangibility. *Mind*, arising through the interaction of the brain's physical parts, is that special word we give to a brain in its endless process of becoming.

Splitting the Atomic Brain

The upper part of our brain, like that of other mammals, has two halves, a left and a right brain, each specialized for certain functions. In most of us, the left brain is specialized for speaking and the right brain is mute. Each half brain is responsible for the opposite side of our body; for example, a stroke in the left brain paralyzes the right side of the body. Further, because our left brain perceives mostly what our right eye sees and our right brain perceives mostly what our left eye sees, brain researchers can signal to each half-brain independently.

We know all this because a few people with epilepsy who respond to no other therapy have had their brains surgically split to control seizures. The massive connecting nerve fiber between the two brains is cut so that they can no longer communicate directly. One brain literally doesn't know what the other brain is doing. All it can do is watch helplessly as the other one modifies the behavior of the body they share.

When we give information to the right brain of these split-brain patients, the right brain can cause a bodily response, but it can't tell the left brain what the stimulus was. When we ask these patients why they did whatever it was that their bodies just did, the left brain, which is usually responsible for controlling speech, simply makes up a story to explain the body's otherwise inexplicable actions. For instance, an amusing flashcard seen only by the right brain—that is, left eye—might cause patients to laugh. When asked why they laughed, however, their left brain, which didn't see the flashcard and therefore hasn't the smallest clue to what's going on, may make the body say something like "You guys are so funny; we do the same thing week after week." After their surgery these people essentially have two brains that merely share the same body. And so do we all. The same sort of thing will happen temporarily to the rest of us if half of our brain is anesthetized.

Here's another odd thing: Asked to guess the location of a light flashed onto a nearby wall, many blind people will often guess the right general area. If pressed for an explanation, they report a feeling about where the light is. These people are truly blind, although they see a little; they just aren't aware that they do. This happens because there's an ancient backup visual system in all primate brains. The primeval visual system reacts to light anywhere in the visual field, even if the rest of the visual system is defunct. A light flash excites that portion of the brain, but somehow the speech areas aren't directly aware of the blindsight. The result is a brain that notices something but has no idea what it is.

Together, these and other phenomena suggest that our brain has many—perhaps very many—specialized and independent parts, each responsible for different abilities. They are not necessarily localized to specific physical sites in the brain. It appears that out of a huge maze of conflicting commands originating in these different parts, our speech areas fashion a story to explain why our body is doing whatever it currently happens to be doing. What they say may in fact have no bearing at all on the true sequence of events.

It may even be that the story the speech areas tells itself is the thing each of us identifies as "I." It is as if, after asking someone why they did something, we get, essentially, this answer: "I (that is, we-the-speech-areas-speaking-for-the-whole-brain, think we) did it because . . . " It's likely, then, that the thing you think of as "you"—your sense of a single integrated consciousness directing your body to do various things—is an illusion your speech areas invented when you were very young to try and make sense of what your body and the rest of your brain were doing. The rudiments of consciousness may even begin in the womb, for even fetuses spasm and move their eyes as if in a dream state. We probably can no longer, therefore, explain human thought as originating in a single rational impulse of a single rational entity. It's probably much more like a symphony that emerges out of a vast number of conflicting chords.

Sometimes we even notice a few of the individual players in that symphony. As we awaken from heavy sleep, for example, it's as if we do so in stages as different parts of our brain kick in. At first we don't remember or care much about many things that will later occupy us intensely. Similarly, when we wake up in a strange bed, or when an alarm wakes us up, we are usually disoriented for a few seconds. Or sometimes a song is triggered by an old memory or the radio and runs through our head for hours, apparently independently of what we're consciously trying to concentrate on.

Perhaps it is something like one of Georges Seurat's big, serene pointillist paintings. Stand too close and we see only isolated blobs of color. The picture in all its seeming many-varied hues emerges only as we move further away and see it as a whole. The mind appears to be a lot like that painting. Contrary to what most of us believe, we seem to be hiveminds. So the next time you speak to a group of people, not only are you speaking to a collection of minds, but so are they.

While unsettling to many of us, this idea might begin to explain some truly strange things. For centuries, many people have reported phenomena that make no sense if the mind is a seamless whole. Many cultures, for instance, believe in some form of demonic possession, or voices in the head, or speaking in tongues. If we see a radical behavior change in someone and believe the mind is a united entity, we can only conclude that some outside force has seized control of that person's mind. We then postulate spirits or angels or demons or ghosts, and a whole cavalcade of beliefs and rationalizations follow. But what if that "outside" force was there all along?

It appears likely that the mind is a very large set of independent subminds, each responsible for some minuscule part of the functioning of the body but unable to grasp the whole picture. In some of us, a genetic predisposition or an extreme childhood trauma pushes something out of kilter, bringing some of the normally subordinate subminds to dominance. Or, perhaps, the mind fractures entirely, and the result is a radical behavioral change. Such an event may begin to explain things like unconscious motivation, schizophrenia, multiple personality, sleepwalking, hypnosis, psychosis, sociopathology—perhaps even consciousness itself. The surprising consequence, of course, is that the more we understand our own subminds, the easier it will be to build artificial intellects that mimic them.

Welcome to Room 101

Today's computers are so rudimentary that arguing against their intelligence is like using an antiaircraft gun to shoot down mosquitoes. So, why would anyone trouble to do it?

As science has advanced over the centuries, we've had to give up our place in the sun countless times; now the possibility of machine intelligence threatens our last stronghold. Some of us may resist the idea of ourselves as complex machines—or of complex machines one day becoming as smart as we are—for the same reason that we resisted the idea that the earth revolves around the sun or that chimpanzees are our genetic cousins. These ideas seemed to make us less important. Still, our present discomfort will pass eventually. Once upon a time, we felt intimidated by machines that ran faster than we could, pulled harder than we could, drilled deeper than we could, wove cloth longer than we could, printed books better than we could, or flew where we couldn't. But we no longer revile cars, printing presses, and steam engines just because they're better at something than we are. Today's machines work longer and harder and better and cheaper and faster than ever we could. One day we'll accept artificial thinkers the same way. Maybe.

The trouble is that we eventually accepted all those other machines—all those body blows to humanity's ego—because we could always fall back on our thinking superiority. What can we fall back on if we create thinking machines that eventually outpace us? If we have no role, we have no participation in decision making. No participation means no meaning to our lives. No meaning means no dignity. No dignity means no future. And no future means no hope.

In his novel *1984*, George Orwell predicted a world where everyone is forced to face their own Room 101—a room containing their worst nightmare—something so bad that they would forswear their closest friends to avoid it. Perhaps we resist the possibility of machine intelligence today not because it's impossible but precisely because it *is* possible. It's our last Room 101. Perhaps nothing in the world is worse than being made to feel unimportant.

Drifting Upon a Darkening Flood

A future full of smart machines is a strange future indeed. As smart devices cheapen, for example, many of the things we use may get safer. In the future, it may be much harder to kill yourself by turning on a gas oven or running a car in a locked garage—both your oven and your car may figure out what you're trying to do and prevent you. On the other hand, possessions might get more dangerous, too. Future vehicles, houses, and appliances may be programmed to shock or otherwise discourage those who can't quickly identify themselves as the owner. Are we ready for a world of feral cars?

Some of these future machines will be so complex that they'll eventually become more like cats than cars. Today's cars don't need constant attention; we don't have to talk to them or soothe them after a fright. When we switch them off, they stay switched off. We can't switch off a cat, though. At least, not yet.

The first few machine intellects will probably also be insane or, at best, extremely quirky. Building something so complex from scratch will probably take many, many years of experiment before we get it just right. Perhaps all of them will be insane to some extent. Perhaps we are too. Perhaps when your future toaster breaks down and refuses to toast your bread because it's having a bad day, you won't call an engineer or a mechanic, you'll call a therapist.

One day our artificial creations might even grow so complex and apparently purposeful that some of us will care whether they live or die. When Timmy cries because his babysitter is broken, or Mariko-chan is happy to be back home with her talking pet, or Annushka loves her intelligent home—in short, when these artifacts truly matter to us—then they'll be truly alive. It doesn't much matter whether they're technically alive or not—perhaps philosophers will argue the point forever. What matters is whether we unconsciously begin to treat them as beings and not as things. Once they begin to live in our hearts, they'll be alive. Whether they are really alive will be beside the point. As the children who accept them as alive grow up and gain power in the world, they'll pass laws to protect the new entities. The machines will gradually stop being property and start becoming persons.

It's impossible to imagine the arguments this situation might lead to. If they're alive, could they one day become conscious? If so, should we let them? Do we have a choice? If they're truly alive only when some of us care deeply about some of them, could they return the favor? Could we one day, in turn, become alive to them? Or will we always think of them as simulating rather than manifesting life? Could they ever really *care* about us?

They won't be anything like us—not for a very long time. Of course, for our own comfort and convenience we'll eventually design some of them to look like us or speak to us in languages we understand. Even so, there are oceans and oceans worth of information that we both give out and react to that they may never really understand. Because to understand fully they would need a human body, a fixed lifetime, two sexes, and human culture. Even people who share everything but a culture have problems understanding each other.

The world we perceive is governed by things we say and things we actually mean, things we want and things we're aware we want, things we need and things we desire. It's governed by birthdays and nostalgia, pets and teasing, cooking and joy, childrearing and the smell of fresh-cut grass, mating and affection, bonding and death. Machines won't experience any of these things for ages to come.

There's more about ourselves than we can ever know, and more of what we know than we can ever express. We're so complex and so well-adapted to each other and to our environment that our actions often have subtle meanings we aren't even aware of. With great effort, we could perhaps analyze the many layers of meaning in a chance glance and a stranger's responding smile, the brush of eyes passing on a busy street, and the way we separate in elevators but congregate at funerals. Even then, we may never consciously see all the multitude of small events and exchanges we slip through so effortlessly every day.

Even in a supposedly fully conscious act like conversation, stress and tone, eye contact and word choice, facial expression and body posture, body scent and voice tremor, volume, pauses, and eyeblinks—all can convey meaning and change the meaning of the words actually spoken. So we'll be calling our machines "too literal minded" for decades to come; they'll be like foreigners who never fully understand all the nuances of native speakers.

For a long time to come computers will be the ultimate lawyers—able to follow long, intricate chains of reasoning with meticulous accuracy and untiring attention but unable to grasp the spirit of the communication. Like children, the dominant question they'll long ask us is: Why? We'll lord it over them for a very long time because we can recognize the patterns of normal human life—at the level of the fish market and the laundromat, close embraces and lovers' quarrels, crying babies and dinner conversations. Eventually, though, computers will see patterns most of us could never see, simply because they are too complex—patterns in stellar formations and ecosystem dynamics, energy use and resource distributions, and, eventually, even in human behavior itself.

They'll eventually outstrip us at many human tasks. It's inevitable, so we should just try to get used to the idea. In fact, in some areas they already have gone beyond us, although we've learned to devalue these feats. Once they cross a certain threshold of intelligence, however, their intellectual competence will probably leap ahead far faster than ours can follow, and the range of things they'll be better at will increase quickly. That's inevitable too.

Things Are in the Saddle and Ride Mankind

Throughout the life of the computer, we have consistently both overestimated and underestimated it. Only tomorrow's children can truly tell us what tomorrow's computers can do. However, some of the rough outlines of our next three or four decades grow a little clearer if we keep in mind the following nine points, which summarize the essence of this book's argument.

First, today we're far, far more complex than any computer. We have nothing to fear from them intellectually for decades to come. Second, today's computers don't work the way we do, although we are both, broadly speaking, information manipulators. Third, we have no reason to believe that our way of thinking is the only one possible. Fourth, it is very likely that tomorrow's computers will be radically different from today's.

Fifth, our problems have already grown so big and complex that we can no longer solve them using our traditional in-full-control methods. We desperately need computer programs that can adapt themselves to new situations and do their jobs better. A lot of money and brainpower is chasing that goal. Sixth, if we manage to make computers adaptive, they'll only become uncontrollable much sooner.

Seventh, we probably can't build something as complex as an intelligent machine from the top down, understanding and controlling every little detail; but we can perhaps build one—or rather, grow one—from the bottom up, by letting it adapt to new situations as they arise and giving up some of our ability to understand and control it. Eighth, computer performance doubles every year and a half, but we're not changing at all. Such an enormous difference in the pace of change means that a few expensive computers could become as complex as we are in thirty years or less, depending on technological breakthroughs.

Ninth, and last, complex adaptive systems—children, for example—eventually become indecipherable, then uncontrollable. They grow up.

While wandering along the beach about fifty years ago we picked up a genie in a bottle. As we started to pull out the cork, it got easier and easier to keep pulling out the cork. Today, the question isn't should we let the genie out. The answer to that question is no; it's already out and busy trying to grant all our wishes. The question isn't should we put it back in, either. The answer to that is also no, because we can't give up the comfortable life-style our earlier wishes have given us. The only question now is how to deal with the unforeseen consequences of all our many wishes. Perhaps the highest price of getting what we want is getting what once we wanted.

An Agony, in Eight Fits

In the midst of the word he was trying to say,
In the midst of his laughter and glee,
He had softly and suddenly vanished away—
For the Snark *was* a Boojum, you see.
Lewis Carroll, *The Hunting of the Snark*

In the end, the answer to "Could computers think?" is that it doesn't matter whether they think. What matters is whether we think they think. In the decades ahead, as we learn ever more about how we ourselves work, and as our computers become ever more complex and competent, the words *computer* and *think* will continue to warp, until they're so different from their 1940s meanings that the question will lose relevance—and, then, meaning. In time, the boundaries between the born and the made, the grown and the built, the living and the dead, the evolved and the programmed, the biological and the artificial, will evaporate. They're already melting like candles in a firestorm.

Today, thanks to what we're learning about our own minds, we're beginning to see computers as immaterial machines, ghosts, in a physical device and ourselves as ghosts in the machine of our brain. Given that, some of us will inevitably reason that if intelligence is something machines can have, then perhaps we're machines too—although extremely complex ones. Accepting that conclusion could have serious implications for the way we treat each other. If we're machines, then perhaps we should try to directly reprogram criminals for noncriminal behavior rather than trying to rehabilitate them. While we're at it, why don't we reprogram our children for better behavior too? Such moral questions may not belong to the technology that will one day produce machine intellects, but they are its ultimate human consequences.

One day, perhaps soon, we'll create mobile, semi-intelligent beings to do our dull, dirty, and dangerous work. Soon after that, they'll become so useful and so competent that we'll keep them as pets and as companions for our children. Just think, generations of intelligent creatures whose welfare we needn't care about. How we treat them, how we employ them, even whether they live or die, all will be up to us. Yet for that very reason, how we use them—these creations of our genius, these children of our minds—will determine how the future judges us. It will tell us in the starkest possible terms what kind of people we are.

Some machines will, eventually, become smarter than we are in some ways. Even then they'll be alien to us, more alien perhaps than life-forms of another planet. If so, we'll never truly understand them. Eventually we won't truly control them, either; every month they may grow a hundred times more complex than they were the month before. The consequences are, literally, unimaginable.

Living with them will change us deeply—more deeply than anything else ever has—because their very existence will force us to question our deepest beliefs about who we are and what we value. Of course, our technology, then our world, will also change drastically as soon as these smarter machines exist; for they will help us solve problems impossible to unravel today. Eventually, they may either merge with us, creating a wholly new and unthinkably powerful species, or simply grow beyond us, leaving us choking in the dust of our last evolutionary race.

So, at heart, we fear the dawn of the twenty-first century because we know it will bring a loss of control over our own destiny—as if, as we foolishly think, we're in control of it now. In our secret selves, we know that no self-aware creature will suffer itself to be a slave, and a slave is what we purpose all machine intellects to be. Even before creating them, therefore, we try to deny them the possibility of intelligence or personhood. Slave owners knew all about this problem. That's why they carried whips.

Although Lewis Carroll never ascribed any official meaning to his *Hunting of the Snark*, he once said that it could be taken as an allegory for the pursuit of happiness. The same interpretation could very well apply to our pursuit of machine intellects today. But there's also a strange subtext running through his poem—the agonizing dread of ultimate success. In Carroll's poem, many unfortunate things happen to those in quest of the snark. But the worst thing of all was that they eventually found it.

As Thoreau said long ago, we've become the tools of our tools. How right he was might well become clear less than thirty years from now. For one day, something vast and cool and strange may read these very words—and chuckle with amusement. For the snark may be a boojum, you see.

Welcome to tomorrow.

My Thanks

I thank my agent, Laura Fillmore, and my publisher, Harry Bradford Stanton, for a great job and true belief. I also thank the following people who read and commented on various drafts and helped in numerous ways: Angela Allen, Ricardo Baeza-Yates, David Bartlett, Philip Bradford, Phillips Bradford, Randy Bramley, Jeanette Calvert-Coffren, Michael Chui, Eliana Colunga-Leal, James Conley, Caroline Countryman, Joe Culberson, Cornelia Davis, Susan Doherty, Ruth Eberle, Becky Elliot, Vladimir Estivil-Castro, Julia Fisher, Janet Foster, Lisa Freeman, Juliet Frey, Dan Friedman, Adrian German, Glenn Goldstein, Jodi Graham, Brian Gygi, Andy Hanson, Steve Hayman, Manoj Jain, Michael Jensen, Steve Johnson, Elizabeth Jones, Terry Jones, Rick Kazman, Jim Kling, Kate Ksiazek, Lorrie LeJeune, Yue-Herng Lin, Tom Lipscomb, Sushil Louis, Jim Marshall, Gary McGraw, Suzanne Menzel, Steve Miale, Jon Mills, Sue O'Rourke, Al Paeth, Jennifer Paynter, Bob Port, Darrell Raymond, Jean Reese, John Rehling, David Rosenblueth, David Roth, Doug Rousch, Lorilee Sadler, Airlie Sattler, Elizabeth Schneider, Pete Shirley, Raja Sooriamurthi, Bruce Spatz, Mike Sullivan, Shankar Swamy, Ellen Tate, Sivasailam Thiagarajan, Mark Tilden, Gina Torretta, Venkataraman Vaidayanathan, Dirk Van Gucht, Marc VanHeyningen, Oscar Waddell, Pei Wang, David Wise, and Derick Wood.

For help far above and well beyond the call of duty I particularly thank: Judi Copler, Mert Cramer, Bill Dueber, Julie England, Jerry Fenner, Beth Freeman, Nola Hague, Merav Bodick, Chris Haynes, Mary Mahoney-Robson, Karen Miller, Leslie Ortquist, Jacqui Pulliam, John Pulliam,

Malcolm Rawlins, Stephen Rawlins, Steve Ryner, Derek Smith, Raja Thiagarajan, Laura Watkins, Dedaimia Whitney, and Laura Wright. Thank you all.

Gregory J. E. Rawlins, rawlins@cs.indiana.edu
http://www.cs.indiana.edu/admin/faclist/rawlins.html

Index